MW00643539

CEASE FIRE

THE STORY OF A SNIPER WHO FOUND LIFE

ABBAS HAMEED *as written by Lisa Lynn Ericson*

CEASE FIRE: The Story of a Sniper Who Found Life
© 2021 Abbas Hameed

All rights reserved. No part of this publication may be reproduced in any form without written permission from Book Villages, P.O. Box 64526, Colorado Springs, CO 80962. www.bookvillages.com

BOOK VILLAGES and the BOOK VILLAGES logo are registered trademarks of Book Villages. Absence of ® in connection with marks of Book Villages or other parties does not indicate an absence of registration of those marks.

All Scripture quotations are taken from THE HOLY BIBLE, NEW INTERNATIONAL VERSION®, NIV® Copyright © 1973, 1978, 1984, 2011 by Biblica, Inc.® Used by permission. All rights reserved worldwide.

ISBN: 978-1-94429-876-0

Cover Design by Scot McDonald
Interior Design by Niddy Griddy Design, Inc.

LCCN: 2021901579

Printed in the United States of America

2 3 4 5 6 7 8 9 10 Printing/Year 25 24 23 22 21

To my beautiful wife, Michelle,
who helped get this book written and published.

Table of Contents

Acknowledgments

Thank you, Lisa Ericson, for writing my story! You are talented at your craft. Michelle and I have enjoyed getting to know you and now consider you a friend to us!

Briggs—Thank you for all your advice writing my story, your cultural understanding, and the snacks!

Karen Pickering—Thank you for helping us publish our book and making our dream come true! We are so thankful for you and your team at Book Villages!

Hameed Christian Ministries board of directors—Thank you for believing in my testimony and your support!

Brian Flewelling and Ken Reinford—Because of meeting with you two at breakfast one morning, my testimony ministry began. I can't thank you enough for your vision and support!

Hameed Christian Ministries financial supporters and prayer team—Thank you for giving financially to help this book become a reality and for all the prayers! May each of you be richly blessed!

Petra Church family—Thank you for your wisdom, encouragement, and opportunities to share my testimony!

Mike and Karissa Gingerich—Thank you so much for helping us with the website and keeping it running smoothly! We appreciate you!

Tammy Sauder—Thank you for babysitting our kids so we could get this book finished.

My kids, Asher and Grace—Thanks for letting Daddy share his testimony with others! I love you to the moon and back!

My Mom and siblings—Thank you for your support and my childhood memories! I miss each one of you!

My Dad—Thank you for your testimony, which changed my life. I'll see you again one day in heaven. I love you and miss you!

Third Brigade Combat Team, 2-505 Eighty-Second Airborne and 101st Airborne Third Battalion, 320th Field Artillery Regiment "Red Knight Rakkasans"—Thank you for trusting me, teaching me, and accepting me as one of your own. I miss you guys!

Jesus Christ—Thank you for putting Christlike men in my life to be a godly example. Without you, I don't have a testimony. Thank you for saving my soul and my physical body. I am still amazed at what you have done! All the glory to God!

CHAPTER ONE

I was unarmed, only a boy, unaware of the battles ahead, unaware that one day I would become a sniper. I would be the sniper who survived. Years later as a ruthlessly resolute sniper, an ace at brandishing a rifle and pistol, I would suddenly be lying flat on the ground, my body covered with charred debris and the raw, pulpy remains of a terrorist. The smoky air contaminated with the stench of burned flesh and fuel surging through my lungs would assure me that I was alive.

But on this brilliant, breezy spring day, I was still a boy, playing on the banks of the Tigris River, famed for its tigerlike swiftness, not even knowing how to swim, wishing I could catch a fish with my bare hands. I did not care about guns—I only wanted to catch my target. Eating the fish was not the goal—catching it was an end in itself. The shore of the river was a natural playground for my older brother Babr and me, just paces away from our home in Samarra, Iraq. The scorching sunlight seemed to soften at the water's edge, and it was the ideal spot to expend some of our boyish energy. Tromping barefoot through the muddy grasslands and splashing in the water were so much better than sitting in a classroom at school. Outside in the open air there were no rules of engagement, the unfaltering arc of the sun the only glimmer of self-restraint. Boyish freedom was the order of the day.

My brother Babr decided to teach me how to swim that afternoon, demonstrating a few basic strokes. He was only one year older than me but already knew how to navigate the waters. I eagerly imitated his motions, barely staying afloat but determined to glide just like him. After a quick lesson, my brother went to join his friends, leaving me in the shallow meadowlands at the shoreline with strict instructions not to venture into the deeper water. My feet sunk into the mud as I stood watching Babr swim farther into the river, and my mind wandered as lazily as the water lapping against the reeds.

A fish caught my attention. My eyes followed its dark, greenish-grey form slithering beneath the surface of the water, and I lifted one foot at a time from the gluey mud, edging mischievously toward my prey. I wanted to catch it, this enemy that was luring me farther from the shore. Lunging for the elusive fish, I lost my footing, oblivious to how far I had strayed from the place where I had stood among the grasses. The fish darted beyond my grasp, and the water was deep.

Submerging in the current, I flailed my arms, forgetting everything that my brother had just taught me about how to swim, gasping for breath out of desperation as I felt death's drowning choke. Babr heard my commotion, speeding through the water to the rescue. He grabbed my thrashing body and pulled me to the shore while scolding me for my witless naughtiness. Feeling the scratch of prickly turf beneath my back as he tugged me out of the swirling eddy, I relaxed, and then stretched out in the sandy mud, relieved. My breathing steadied, and as the water droplets on my skin evaporated in the sun's strong rays, I was glad to be alive.

It had only been a scare, and I was fine, though the day's adventure had other painful consequences. Before Babr and I walked home, his friends hurried ahead, telling my doting mother what had happened. What to them was great gossip, to my mother was a terrible telegram. When we arrived at the house, she met us not with a reassuring embrace but, instead, with a water hose, poised to give us a good beating. Lashing our suntanned, impish bodies with the snakelike hose, my mother reinforced a lesson that stayed with me forever—the value of following orders. It stung. As my finger traced the raised, red welts that the hose had stamped on my skin, I knew that I had disobeyed, treading where I did not belong, yet I knew that she loved me.

My earliest childhood memory, however, was even more stinging than that escapade along the Tigris River. I still remember a day when I was only eight or nine years old, caught up in a swirl of revenge and suffering the consequences for something that I had not done at all. Being the son of my father brought benefits, for sure, but also challenges. Although he was a man of many noble qualities, he made some choices that affected our entire family. One of those choices involved a woman who was not my mother. It was a fleeting, adulterous affair that I will never forget.

My mother had just given birth to my younger sister, so there were four of us siblings at the time: my oldest sister Nadira, my brother Babr, baby Nafisa, and me, the third in line. My father met a nurse at the hospital during the delivery, and the flirtatious attention that he gave her was a disgrace to the family. Upholding the honor of a family's name is so fundamental in Iraqi society that my mother's relatives intervened, rejecting my father for his wayward whims. In a bewildering sequence of events, my perfidious father and the nurse started to live under the same roof, and my two older siblings and I were compelled to stay with them in a house that was not our own. My mother's family reclaimed her and the newborn baby girl, enclosing them far from us, far beyond where her bonds of love could reach me.

No one was happy, and an undercurrent of dysfunction and revenge pervaded the family structure. I was devasted, yanked away from my mother's loving arms. My father's concubine, the nurse, tried to appease me with niceties. She fed me sandwiches in an attempt to soothe my angst, but I rejected her food, not wanting anything to do with her. As a result, my father whipped me with his prayer beads, and I wrestled with a new reality where faith and love were misconstrued all around me. Extended family members hurled dead cats and the rotted, reeking carcasses of other animals onto the nurse's property, taking matters into their own hands with undisguised rancor. It was horrible and unbearable for her—and for us as children.

When my sister, brother, and I whimpered in despair, some relatives came to the nurse's house and punished us for crying. One day, they locked the three of us in a small shower room, only six feet square, which made us wail even more frantically. One undue, unjustified punishment led to another and another. To muffle our crying, they torturously plunged us headfirst into enormous water barrels which seemed like abysmal lakes of tears. Unable to swim, I could barely breathe in my anguish. The abusive ordeal was threatening, but we all survived unscathed. Eventually, the nurse became so disgusted with the scenario that she broke off all relations with my father, demanding that he leave her alone.

I was too young to understand what was happening. All I knew was that, eventually, we were back at home with my mother and father, just like before the episode of marital disloyalty. The memory of that water barrel remained riveted in my mind and, with it, a childlike thirst, an awareness of revenge. Only later would I learn more about battles and victories, both personal and on a much larger scale. And only later would my nightmarish helplessness in the water seem as child's play compared to the torrent of terrors I would face in wartime.

CHAPTER TWO

Samarra, Iraq, a city about two hours northwest of Baghdad, was a good place to call home, even if I was a bit of a misfit. I was born there on November 19, 1983, joining my two older siblings in a comfortable home on the outskirts of the city, a large house tended by a housekeeper, with several vehicles parked on the property. It was safe, and we could wander to the Tigris River or throughout the neighborhood, more interested in our spirited antics than in learning about the archeological treasures of the UNESCO World Heritage site beneath our feet. Samarra had once been a preeminent Islamic capital city, but I was just a boy exploring the pastimes of the present, not the legacy of the past. The pomegranate trees in the yard offered their luscious, ruby-red fruit and flecked shade from the sun, their broken branches occasionally serving as whips when I misbehaved. Even if I flinched when my mother would punish me, she always disciplined me with love, saying, "I only beat you because I want you to become better, a good boy, a good man."

I was a misfit because of my heritage, not understanding the larger picture of religious history. I only knew that I was like a smudge in the portrait of the society that surrounded me. My mother was Sunni Muslim, while my father was Catholic, both of them Iraqi. My father had blue eyes and a white complexion, as the grandson of a British farmer who had settled long ago in the Ad-Dawr area of Iraq and married a local Muslim woman. In a culture where the concept of "an eye for an eye" is taken literally, life becomes susceptible not only to jealousy but also to justice and the value of upholding the honor of a family name. Before I was born, my British great-grandfather was killed, his death serving as devastating evidence that the people in the community did not think highly of the wealth that this non-Muslim foreigner was gathering in their midst. The tragedy sparked a cycle of revenge that continued beyond his generation, resulting also in the murder of my grandfather. My father was only a newborn when his father's life was cut short, and his Muslim mother abandoned him to be raised by an aunt who had never married. When he was a teenager, he became a nominal Catholic, struggling to find his identity in a society where his white skin stood in stark contrast to everyone else.

My father's Catholicism did not prevent him from marrying my mother and establishing a home that was, by all appearances, Muslim. Religion was not important in our household, although my mother did attempt to maintain some semblance of Muslim rituals in the home. The calls to prayer reverberated five times each day throughout the city of Samarra, radiating solemnly from the towering minarets, but no one in our house was devout enough to respond. During the monthlong Ramadan fast, we would deprive ourselves of food during the daytime for the first week and then loosen our faithfulness as the month continued. I remember getting caught sneaking a bite to eat, hiding next to the refrigerator until my mother noticed my small frame crouched down, chewing. I remember catching my mother doing the same, sipping some water when it was forbidden. But, despite a lack of strict devotion in our home, my mother was careful to raise me with a good conscience and high moral values, teaching me not to steal, teaching me to treat people as I would want to be treated. When I was about ten years old, I started going to the local mosque, wanting to please and honor my mother as she tried to guide us in a way that would demonstrate respect for her scrupulously religious father. She never forced me to go, desiring only that I would learn how to live a good life and not provoke a curse of shame on our bloodline. Mostly, I went to the mosque to observe with mild curiosity the rituals of men who would pray seemingly incessant prayers to Allah. I watched with fascination as they tapped their knees with their fingers each time they spoke the name of Allah, seeking to glorify him with the increasing tally. Their formal observance meant nothing to me except that it became familiar, the religion of our environment, the culture that was mine by default. Like any good Iraqi, my birth certificate stated that I was Muslim, and I accepted it naturally.

If religion was familiar but vague, even more familiar was the conflict between my father and mother. As a child, I watched their explosive arguments that nearly crossed the line into domestic violence. But that, too, was a normal feature of Iraqi culture. My father was in charge of the house, and my mother knew it. His requirements reigned with no questions allowed. I never saw him lay a hand on my mother, although sometimes he tried. Once when he was verbally threatening her and ordering her to submit to his will, she picked up a water pipe, saying, "I dare you to come." My father walked away.

Their marital quarrels were moderate compared with what I saw in other relationships, where men would hit their wives for the smallest acts of disobedience. Not complying with the full expectations of domestic duties could incur as a minimum a beating or—worse—a stoning. Even my own distant cousins would throw stones at their wives if they failed to do enough manual labor on the family farm. These squabbles disturbed me, stirring in me a desire to defend the honor and dignity of women. It was not a climate of tender gentleness between man and wife, and it haunted me years later during my military service. Sometimes while out on patrol, I would see a man exerting violence upon a woman, and it would trigger a flashback of what I had observed in my youth. In moments like this, vivid recollections and livid rage would crescendo within me. I would tell my commanding officer to stop the vehicle. Taking matters into my own hands, I would approach the offending man and smack him in the face, saying, "This is how your wife feels." For better or for worse, my home life nurtured in me a desire to defend what is right.

Not only did my father not exhibit much tenderness toward my mother, but also, he was firm and emotionally aloof with me. Affirmation was not the norm. I would get slapped on the back of the head if my performance was not good enough, or sometimes it was a stare that simply communicated, "You had better do this, or else." Once, my father was showing me how to fix a PVC water pipe, and when I repeatedly failed to meet his standards, he grabbed the pipe and hit me in the head. His treatment was never too severe, however. I tried my best to fulfill his requests, always wishing he would call me Apsi, the nickname he used when I had done a good job.

Authority was significant, affection was subtle, rewards were dispersed without drawing attention to the giver or the recipient. We had a small, cold storage room in the house where my father would deposit bags of oranges, potatoes, onions, items that he purchased as ample supplies for the family. The best were the candy bars, tucked away in the storage room out of reach of the children. After me, there were six more brothers and sisters, for a total of nine children in the family, each of us quite close in age. My mother was the one who would quietly place a chocolate treat on the nightstand near my bed if I had done well in school, heartily distributing what my father had bought. Because these gestures came from my mother's hands, it was her love that I felt the most.

It was my father's non-Iraqi bloodline that became a source of irritation for me personally, along with his embarrassing activities that caused us to be the brunt of local ridicule. Instead of affection for him, a root of distaste grew in my heart as a child. The boys in school started hassling and bullying my siblings and me for having a white father, typical youthful taunting that seems dismissible but cuts to the core of a child's self-worth. The aggravation worsened when my father's business began to falter, requiring intensive, laborious effort to maintain the high standard of wealth that he desired. The pressures of providing for his family weighed heavily on my father, and my inner impression of being around him became increasingly sour. He would step out of the house in a cloud of internal turmoil, going to bars and hotels in Baghdad, where he would drink alcohol and mingle with people who were a bad influence on his character. Alcohol, while overtly forbidden in Iraqi Muslim culture, was covertly mishandled, often polluting the semblance of professed piety in the community. Within about a year, the police were regularly attempting to arrest my father for fights and perhaps other illicit acts associated with his wild lifestyle. He would always tell them that he was related to Saddam Hussein's second-in-command, managing to be spared while they arrested the bartender or someone else. However, after a while, the police realized that he was lying, and they initiated another routine—putting him in jail. Because he still had a lot of money, my father would exert his leverage to be released.

This dismal cycle, in and out of prison, continued nearly twenty times, and my school classmates knew about my father's tarnished reputation. I still have a scar on my head from one of the stones that the boys threw at me in jest, a brutal teasing for something that was out of my control. Rather than crumple and cry in front of them, I learned to stand tall, hurling stones in re-taliation and defending myself. If the insults overpowered me, my brother Babr would help. Unfortunately, these playground fights soon became the norm, and I developed a tough heart, glad that my skin was olive-toned and my eyes dark, like my mother's. I was determined to be a strong Iraqi boy.

CHAPTER THREE

L ife at home with so many siblings was animated, at times
hectic, yet also peaceful and comfortable, even if always with
an air of the unexpected. I never knew what my unpredictable,
ambitious father would do next, but that uncertainty was not
necessarily negative. One evening, when I was fourteen, my
father called us at the house in Samarra, announcing that he was
bringing home a surprise. All of us children were excited, hardly
knowing what he had said, but hearing the vigor in his voice. Since
his business dealings and legal troubles caused a distance between
us, the prospect of a surprise was even more special.

Suddenly, the large metal gate in the front of our property
opened with a loud, toilsome screech, and my father arrived in a
truck, along with a band of deftly spry Bedouin shepherds and a
flock of 250 griping sheep. They scattered all over our front yard,
penned in by the concrete wall that surrounded the property, and
the chaos was such that we struggled to open the front door to run
outside. Within moments, there were sheep wandering inside the
house, some even giving birth in the kitchen. We rallied together as
a family to make some order out of the mess, opening the kitchen
window to pass the lambs to someone else standing in the yard. I
had never gotten that close to a sheep, and before I knew it, I was
cleaning up their droppings on the floor. As the ruckus droned on
for hours, the neighbors began to complain about the deafening
bleating, and our own excitement faded into annoyance because

of all the work this surprise had dumped upon us. Two days later, my father sent the sheep away with the Bedouin men, and I never learned what had motivated such a spontaneous delivery of sheep to our house. Perhaps it was an indication of my father's volatile lifestyle, a warning that I did not know how to decipher.

One week later, we had another surprise, much grimmer. Instead of a truckload of sheep, three armored secret service vehicles with tinted windows cruised to a halt in front of our house. My mother was at work in a new position at a pharmaceutical manufacturing company, while my father and the rest of us siblings were home, oblivious to the pending intrusion. Instantly, armed men in black uniforms burst through the door on a stinging mission. They were searching for my father. Neither he nor any of us knew why this was happening. Shaken, my father hastily tried to hide in a spare room among a pile of extra blankets and mattresses, while my older brother and I remained in the main hall, pretending to be brave and attempting to protect our family from these intimidating men. It was to no avail. Within moments, the guards dragged my father away from the storage room. As he passed us in the entryway, my father spoke in the strongest tone he could muster, "It is OK, kids."

It was not OK. The guards who arrested my father snatched him away with no explanation, and only much later did we learn what had prompted their alarming actions. For six months, we did not know if he was dead or alive. We searched for him every day, going from one police station to another to inquire about any trace of the father of our family, the head of our household. Finally, at one police station we heard the sobering truth.

My father had supposedly been conducting business with a woman, and one night they went out drinking. A few drinks evolved into a fling in a hotel room where the alluring woman deceived him. While my father was intoxicated, the woman stole a blank check that he had already signed. Pre-signing checks was a normal practice for him, a token of wealth at an auction to validate his bid. Writing the check payable to herself for a large sum of money, the woman then went to the bank and tried to cash it. She knew that he was wealthy, but she overestimated the amount of funds available, and the check bounced. In Iraq, a check with insufficient funds is punishable with a prison sentence, and the woman was too sly to allow any blame to fall upon her own record. Instead, she took advantage of her connections to implicate my father and called upon a friend who was linked to Saddam Hussein's authoritative oldest son, Uday. He dispatched his personal security guards to arrest my father, and a neighbor claimed to have spotted Uday himself through the windshield of one of the vehicles that parked in front of our house that fateful day.

My father was sentenced to six years in prison, a punishment that combined the crime of a bad check and the accumulated wrongdoing of previous incidents of lying about being a relative of Hussein's second-in-command. The government seized my father's properties, including five houses, two brand-new cars, and three dump trucks—plus the 250 sheep that he had acquired only a week before his arrest. The pendulum from wealth to indigence had swung wide, leaving us suspended in a predicament of loss. My mother's job at the pharmaceutical company entitled her to a house, and we were able to live there when everything else was taken. Disoriented and stripped of our father, at least we were not homeless.

As soon as my father's six-year sentence was official, my family hired a lawyer to fight his case, discovering a bleak reality. In Iraq, as in so many parts of the world, money is the fuel of influence. The lawyer recommended that we present two million Iraqi dinar, an amount equivalent to about $2,000 in US currency. We were unable to pay such a high price, having been deprived of our assets, so we asked my father's relatives to contribute their agricultural earnings. Some donated willingly, while others shared money on the condition that we would repay them. Once we gave the stipulated amount to the government, my father's sentence was reduced to three years.

Destitute, my father was tortured by the prison guards. In the winter, he was permitted only icy cold showers, and in the summertime, the water was scalding hot. The guards flogged him, taking him to the execution room and putting a noose around his neck as a scare tactic. He complied with their orders, not wanting to aggravate his status, while at the same time the underpaid guards ate the food that would have been his nourishment.

As if his imprisonment were not grueling enough, one of my father's estranged relatives spread a false rumor that he was a drug dealer and had hidden money somewhere inside our house. The imaginary story surrounding my father's activities spread, and thieves began to attack our house in the middle of the night, trying to locate the nonexistent money. A well-meaning relative on my mother's side of the family rigged our door handles with electrical hot wires as a deterrent to thieves. One rainy night when the door handle was charged with 220 volts, a money-hungry intruder was jolted by the shock, falling to the ground and then escaping out of sight. The body print of the would-be robber was still in the mud when we opened the door the following morning. In hindsight, it was almost amusing, although at the time it was terrifying. A respite in the midst of these attacks was the friendship that we developed with a Kurdish family next door who owned many goats and sheep. The children would jump over the fence to play hide and seek in the yard with us while their father was at home, a kidney disease preventing him from being more active. Each of us needed to find some diversion from the concerns that were beyond our years to resolve.

Tough as I may have seemed on the exterior, I also welcomed the occasional opportunity to escape from the disputes in Samarra. Sometimes while my father was in prison, we would go to the desert farm in Ad-Dawr where he was raised, about forty minutes away from our home. My assignment was to help with the farm animals, especially the sheep. Even though they were not smart creatures, I enjoyed the sheep's company, far away from the bullying and raucous jeering of my classmates who were all too aware of my father's imprisonment. At first, the sheep would be hesitant to follow me, but after a few days they would trail along through the dry turf as I led them to pasture. My playful spirit would surge, free from the constraints of the classroom, and I would trick the silly sheep, hiding in a ditch when they were not watching. They would look around, bleating like a crazed flock, worried and wondering where I had gone. By all appearances, they were vulnerable to attack, but I was nearby, scrambling out of the ditch and whistling to attract their attention. They would pad along behind me, their foolish little brains relieved and their parched tongues thirsty for water pumped from the desert well. Leading those dim-witted, dirty sheep to pasture and water was a refreshing interlude that became imprinted forever in my memory. In later years I would value even more the duties of a shepherd, while at the time I was more concerned about the chasm between me and my father.

The prison permitted visitors once per month, only on weekends. As a young teenager, seeing my father in prison was tortuous to my impressionable mind, my image of fatherhood dimming with the experience. Even getting close to him was a challenge. My brother Babr and I went to the prison and were nearly trampled in the hallways by a throng of Shia ladies dressed in black. We quickly climbed the walls like monkeys, trying to avoid the crowd of distraught visitors crammed into a tight space. Every weekend, there were typically two to three deaths among the visitors due to trampling. The effort was worth it to me, not only to remind my father that his family had not abandoned him, but also to learn from his perspective, molded in the cruel walls of prison. My father's humbled condition prompted him to confess his poor behavior to us personally. He divulged the account of his drunken stupor, expressing deep regret for his infidelity. "I am not worthy to ask for your forgiveness," he told my mother, and she accepted his heartfelt apology. And because of his deliberate good behavior as a prisoner, he was released six months before completing his reduced three-year sentence.

The relief was short-lived. Within less than a year, my father was back in prison. This time, the government found him guilty of being a draft dodger, never having completed the mandatory three years of service in the Iraqi Army, a requirement for all men once they reach age eighteen. He had only served for several months during the Iran-Iraq War of the 1980s, deserting the military and blemishing his registry. He was sentenced to an underground prison for one year, locked in complete darkness. Once a day, the guards brought him outside for two minutes of sunlight, a meager solace in the midst of the blackout that blanketed his life. Throughout his sentence, he had no shower and was merely given a scant amount of water when he needed to relieve himself. Only my mother and my older sister, Nadira, visited him during his confinement, attempting to deliver clothes and sustenance. The guards kept everything for themselves, and my father barely had enough food and drinking water.

With his underhanded life unveiled in the dark and humid subterranean prison, my father called out to the God of the entire Earth in agony, recalling what he had learned as a teenager when he turned to Catholicism. The crisis prodded him to dig deeper. It was the genuine faith of a broken man, and God not only brought him out of the underground prison after his one-year sentence but also nurtured a new attitude in his spirit. When he was released, my father was a renewed man, grateful to see the sun and smiling in a way that I had never seen. He immediately devoted himself to hard work so that he could provide for the family, and he was a noticeably selfless man. His happiness was uncanny, and I gravitated to him more than in all of my youth, even though I was becoming a man.

I was eighteen years old when my father rejoined the family

after the tormenting imprisonment. One week after his release, my father invited me to join him on a clothes shopping outing. We had never gone shopping together, nor had we ever spent a day alone as father and son. At first, I was cautious, not knowing how to interact with my ex-convict father, and nervous that I might say something that could upset him. I was unsure if his brighter countenance was a passing breeze, and I did not want to stir up any storm clouds. But my worry faded as my father acted very much at ease, talking openly in between shops, admitting his mistakes. At one store, he insisted on buying me a sweater, a smart style in soft brown and green tones, the tag on the collar indicating that it was a beautiful article of Iraqi craftsmanship. His gift embraced me so much that I still keep that sweater in perfect condition to this day.

As I walked with him along the city streets, my hands full with the purchases, my ears eager to hear every morsel that my father wanted to share, he stopped abruptly on the street. A homeless man sat at his feet, leaning against a telephone pole, tattered clothing and dim eyes betraying his poverty. Before I hardly knew what was happening, my father was taking off his classy *dishdasha* man-dress, an appalling act for any honorable Iraqi man. Stripped of the dignified grey dishdasha, my father stood on the sidewalk in only his diminutive underpants. It was improper, scandalous. Then he gave the dishdasha to the outcast man. People passed by the unsightly scene, gaping, not sure if they should stare at my father or look at the disgraceful homeless man whose dreary eyes now brightened behind tears of gratitude. My embarrassment soon turned to pride, remaining next to my father and witnessing the astounding generosity from one formerly destitute man to another. How could this man who had once been so self-engrossed now be giving his own stylish clothing away to a shabby stranger?

"What are you doing?" I asked my father.

"He needs these clothes more than I do," he answered.

Surely, prison had done something to my father. Or maybe it was God. A voice inside of me prodded me to pray. Praying to

God, praying to Allah—all of it was foreign to me. My shock at my father's transformation stirred me to consider that perhaps God really does exist. And I silently prayed, "God, if you truly exist, don't punish me like you did my father, but help me to be the man you want me to be."

CHAPTER FOUR

As my father was finishing his prison term, I had completed high school and turned eighteen, the age of military service. There was no doubt that I would fulfill this mandatory expectation, especially after observing the severity of my father's punishment for evading his responsibilities. When registering, I had the option of joining the Iraqi Army for three years in the desert or becoming a police officer for five years in the city. I had heard ghastly stories about rape in the army and about new recruits being forced to bring their sisters to be sexually exploited by army officers. The choice to become a police officer was clear, even if it meant a five-year commitment.

For two months, I attended the police academy in Tikrit, the hometown of Saddam Hussein, a dull regimen where I sat around for hours, with little tangible training. I mastered the art of saluting while holding an AK-47 but never once learned how to shoot a gun. Crawling through mud was the peak of my activity, not exactly what I had envisioned as an incoming member of the police force. I thought I would hit the city streets in uniform and be a model of citizenship, esteemed by pedestrians passing me on the sidewalk and, more specifically, maybe even admired by the girls. When I received my academy graduation certificate, the rite of passage came to an abrupt halt. Although I had signed a paper committing to five years of service, that time frame had been surreptitiously changed. In bold letters, the certificate stated that

I was bound to twenty-five years of active duty as a police officer for the Republic of Iraq.

"How did this change?" I asked the officials, attempting to convey enough respect to mask my astonishment.

"If you do not want to serve, we will just put you in prison," they replied, allowing no discussion.

I was upset but did not dare to exhibit my annoyance for fear of being killed by the government. Later, out of view, I expressed my frustration by soaking my certificate with water and shredding it. My father, however, saw what I had done. Wise after suffering in prison for his own foolishness, he said, "Do not be silly. They have a copy."

He was right, and I knew I had to comply. I showed up at the largest police headquarters in Tikrit, ready to honor my obligation to the Iraqi government. The authorities assigned me to guard the station at night and deliver documents to the courthouse during the day. Knowing that Hussein's domineering relatives lived in Tikrit aggravated the seriousness of my new post. They had complete liberty to live as they pleased, even if it infringed on the law. It was terrifying. When one of Hussein's relatives would arrive at the station, wildly drunk, the older Kurdish officers would spare me the nervous encounter, sending me to another side of the building out of range of the agitation. I greatly trusted these Kurdish men, welcoming their counsel as I adapted to my role.

Soon, I transferred to the investigation and interrogation team, no longer running courthouse errands. The honor of increased responsibility brought with it the harsh reality of my duties. Under Hussein's regime, interrogations escalated to brutality toward any suspects, and our police station was no exception.

One day, we arrested a Bedouin man, the stump of his middle finger incriminating him in a horrific homicide, as one of the bullets from his gun had ricocheted and damaged his hand. He could not hide the evidence of what he had done. The Iraqi police typically avoid intervening in tribal affairs, but this Bedouin had taken more than "an eye for an eye" in an extreme act of revenge. Shooting to kill, when in defense of the family, is considered acceptable, but not battering another man with repeated bullets after he is already dead. The Bedouin had shot his adversary with three AK-47 magazines, each containing thirty bullets, a level of violence that we could not overlook.

We pressured our closemouthed captive, beating him so that he would confess his crime. When our initial constraints were met with stubborn silence, we intensified the approach. As the man lay with his back on the floor, we threaded his feet through the sling of an AK-47 and then twisted the rifle to tighten the strap so that he could not move. I was one of two officers who held the AK-47 high in the air so that the suspect's legs were perpendicular to the floor. A third interrogating officer then lashed the suspect's feet with an electrical cable in order to elicit a confession. In the ferocity of the moment, the cable swung wide and slapped my arm. The pain was horrendous, much worse than my mother's water hose whippings, and I flinched, requesting permission to exit the room while I recovered. That brief thirty minute interlude changed my perspective.

When I was summoned to return to my position in the interrogation room, I refused. Claiming that I was still hurt, I voiced my objection, expressing my aversion to such inhumane treatment of any suspect. At that, the lieutenant colonel issued a new command, sending me to prison for three days as a punishment for disobeying his orders. By a twist of fate, the officers locked me in the same cell as the Bedouin murderer.

Now in my own dungeon, guilty of nothing more than trying to preserve my conscience, I grappled with the strategies of the police force to which I had pledged my loyalty. The Bedouin man who occupied my cell began to divulge the motivation behind the ninety bullets with which he had smattered his antagonist. The man he had killed had taken the life of his beloved teenage brother, a loss that he could not withstand. Each bullet represented the tears that he ached to shed, and now he was guilty of murder. As if the grief of his brother's death was not heartbreaking enough, the torture he endured in the police headquarters made him fearful about the destiny of his entire family, the wife and children he loved. Looking into the eyes of this distraught Bedouin man, I could only remember my father's last words as he was dragged away to prison. "It is OK," my father had said, trying to reassure me as the government guards tightened their firm grip. I knew that things might never be OK for this Bedouin man, and I wished that he could be freed from such heartless torture. Compounding my anguish, I recalled having seen police officers stealing sheep from Bedouins in the community. The swirl of injustice muddied what my mother had taught me about not stealing, about always doing what is right. Upholding the law as a police officer verged on foolishness if we were no longer protecting the people, instead smudging the line between right and wrong. The torture, the stealing, it all conflicted with the image of the man I wanted to become.

But I was obligated to twenty-five years of service as a policeman, and as soon as I was released from those three pensive days of prison, I returned to my duties as an interrogator. Immediately, the lieutenant colonel tested my obedience by ordering me to coerce the naked Bedouin murder suspect to sit forcibly on a glass Pepsi bottle. Imagining his extreme emotional humiliation and physical misery, I refused. I could not fathom inflicting such hardship on my former cellmate, a prisoner whose anguish was all too human. Infuriated, the lieutenant colonel swiftly sent me to prison for another five days.

The year was 2003, and my internal conflict as an imprisoned police officer was a speck on the map of Iraq while a much broader conflict was brewing. In the global arena, a disparity of leadership philosophies was clashing closer and closer to home. And yet, I was unaware, hungry for justice and banished to a small cell for five days. One afternoon, the police station's amiable Kurdish chef brought me a freshly made falafel sandwich, the spicy pickled mango sauce enlivening my languishing taste buds, and his nurturing presence soothing my nerves.

"Abbas, it will be OK," the chef said.

When my father had told me that things would be OK, they were not, but these words seemed different now, coming spontaneously from the mouth of this kindly Kurdish chef. What could he be trying to tell me? I longed to be freed from prison and released entirely from the crushing responsibilities of this oppressive police force. I hated who I was becoming.

"What do you mean?" I asked the chef, chewing the chopped cucumbers and lettuce that mingled deliciously with the seasoned falafel.

Without disclosing any details, he told me what he knew. There were rumors of war, reports that the US military was preparing to invade Iraq. And somehow, he was confident that the international conflict on the horizon would be better for me than the internal conflict I was facing.

CHAPTER FIVE

Promptly upon my release after five days, the police major sent me to the armory room with an air of urgency. I quickly realized that the rumors of war were trumping all activities and that my usefulness to the police force was evolving rapidly. Now I was merely an able-bodied fighter. One of the officers issued me an AK-47 and one magazine, saying, "If you see a US soldier, shoot."

I had never shot a gun before because my training at the police academy had been theoretical, limited to demo pseudo-weapons. However, not knowing how to shoot an AK-47 was a minor detail in comparison with my primary concern.

"No," I said. I did not want to fight against the US military. I greatly respected the United States, and my family had mourned the tragedy of 9/11, turning off the television for a week to muffle the anti-US noise that was skyrocketing in the Middle East. My refusal sparked the fury of the authorities, and they threatened to hang me if I did not fight. Hanging was a palpable possibility in Iraq.

I quickly backtracked, saying that I would accept the gun. Under one condition. I told the officers that if I saw any US soldiers, I would drop the gun and surrender with my hands in the air. My provisional willingness was enough to avert a hanging, and my superiors gruffly ordered me to stand guard at the police station.

That night, the bombings began. The missiles plummeted from thundering jets overhead as I stood guard at the police station, terrified. The impact flashes lit up the black sky as if it were daytime, the shrapnel scattering uncontrollably. Halfway through my shift, another police officer invited me to take refuge through the night at his nearby apartment there in Tikrit, since Samarra was too far away. He assured me that in the midst of the warfare pandemonium, the police major would not even notice my absence if I returned before 6:00 a.m.

However, when I arrived the next morning at my guarding post at 5:34 a.m., the major was waiting for me, steaming like the explosions that echoed throughout the skies. "Traitor!" he shouted, fuming. Through teeth clenched with rage, he told me that I would be hanged that day for aiding the US military instead of defending the Iraqi government. I trembled, waiting for him to take action.

The major then spoke with the lieutenant colonel, repeating his accusation that I was a traitor deserving an abrupt hanging that very day. While I waited for my fate to unfold, the sharp lines of my dark green uniform were no defense against the terror that welled up within me, and I sobbed the salty tears of a soul about to sink into the grave. The lieutenant colonel, the same officer whom I had disobeyed twice when refusing to torture the Bedouin suspect, saw me crumpling. "Come with me," he said, his tone of voice giving no hint of his thoughts.

I followed the lieutenant colonel as he walked briskly toward the major, stopping in front of him. "You should be ashamed of yourself," the lieutenant colonel shouted in strong Arabic. To my astonishment, he was cursing at the major, not me. I stood back and watched as the lieutenant colonel lifted one hand and struck the major back and forth on both cheeks, the *beep* slap, as we call it in the police force. The lieutenant colonel then announced to the major that he would be hanged with Saddam. As for me, my next orders were straightforward—return to my post as a guard at the police station. With my impending execution dismissed, I felt a staggering excitement that surpassed my comprehension. But this was wartime, with no time for reveling in the most basic thrill of still being alive.

The bombs continued to whirl overhead, rattling and twirling through the air on their snaky trail to the ground, buffeting the surface with one blaring boom after another. One of the missiles weaseled down the road in front of the police station, halting abruptly when it hit a telephone communication center and erupting with volcanic madness. The intimidating force of the US military prompted feelings of powerlessness in all of us, and throughout the ensuing two weeks, Iraqi police officers started to flee, running for their lives. In the midst of the disarray, the major raided the armory room, stole a stash of weapons, and escaped from his pending hanging. The Kurdish chef disappeared. I was torn, hoping that the US military would put an end to Hussein's regime and the evil that raged throughout Iraq while also fearing that one of their bombs would pulverize my earnest desire to become a good man.

On one of those volatile days when the bombings blurred the outlook of even the sturdiest officers, I noticed my mother's second cousin, a police sergeant named Jabar, leaving with a duffel bag. We did not know each other well, but no branch of the family tree is too spindly in wartime, especially in Iraq, where family roots extend deeply into the landscape of society. "Where are you going?" I asked him.

Telling me that he was abandoning his post, Jabar added, "Do you want to stay or go?"

"I want to go," I replied impulsively, my bravado disintegrating into a desperate desire to take refuge.

"Come on, let's go," Jabar urged. Before following him, I hastily dashed to the vacant ball field next to the police station, burying my AK-47 and police identification badge in a pile of dirt. Jabar ushered me quickly to a commercial box truck where a man sat behind the wheel in a hurry to complete his delivery route, now with two passengers. Jabar sat in the cabin next to the driver, while

I climbed into the freezer compartment in the back, discovering that my riding companions would be bags and bags of frozen chickens. The driver turned off the refrigeration unit so that I would not freeze, and throughout the forty-five minute drive, the putrid stench of slaughtered poultry clouded my impressions of life itself during the spontaneous getaway. They dropped me off at my parents' house in Samarra, my relief to be welcomed home intermingling with the surrealistic experience of burning my police uniform in the yard outside our house. The flames swallowed up the fabric, engulfing within seconds the balance of twenty-five years that I no longer owed to the government.

The atmosphere of uncertainty muted my thoughts and aspirations. I remember little about that first day home. Two days later, my father woke me up, animatedly shooing me to the front door of our house to see what was happening.

Throngs of people teemed in the streets of Samarra, applauding as an imposing convoy of US soldiers trekked through the city. These were the men of Operation Iraqi Freedom, invaders who were received as heroes by my fellow countrymen. The elated crowd threw flowers, chilled Pepsi cans, and cigarettes at the soldiers, tokens of gratitude for the renewed hope that was spreading throughout the land. It was the spring of 2003, and I was oblivious to the international media footage showing citizens of Iraq toppling the statue of Saddam Hussein in Baghdad. Samarra was my world, and it was changing in front of my eyes.

CHAPTER SIX

Within about a month, the same distant cousin Jabar called me with a question that seemed to be the exact opposite of what had just transpired. "Do you want to return as a police officer?" he asked, a prospect that seemed absurd to me.

"No, I do not want to serve for twenty-five years. I am done," I answered, at once assertive and confused.

"Things are different now," Jabar said. He explained that there was no need for a twenty-five year commitment. The US military had overtaken Iraq; the existing police force had been abolished. I would be working alongside US soldiers.

"Will I be paid?" I asked.

"Yes," Jabar replied, "with American dollars." The paltry Iraqi dinars that I had been earning were only the equivalent of $2 per month. I thanked Jabar for the idea, intrigued enough to ask my father for advice. He encouraged me to try it, saying that I could always return home if I did not like working with the US soldiers. Remembering the victorious convoy that had just paraded down our street, my admiration for the US military swelled, and I longed to join their brave feats.

I returned to the police station in Tikrit that I had ditched, holding my chin up as I submitted my name to enlist. The US military police assigned me to serve as a security officer, guarding the station. When one of the American captains realized that I spoke decent English, he asked me to act as an interpreter. I had studied British English in school for eight years, and although

I did not feel fluent, my proficiency and Arabic knowledge were considered valuable to military police communications. I assisted by familiarizing the US military with Tikrit and the larger surrounding area, identifying routes, pointing out where Hussein's relatives lived, and providing tips about which pockets of the region were pro-Saddam. It was an abrupt about-face, positioning me alongside the foreigners who had intervened in the tumultuous country that I called home. To some, I was considered a traitor. To me, I was coming of age as a man.

However, this was not about me, nor a placid linguistic exercise as an interpreter. This was war. In those first few weeks, I was selected to accompany the US soldiers on missions, translating, advising about Iraqi culture, and significantly influencing their strategies. They relied on me to identify Fedayeen, a ramshackle assortment of orphans in their mid-teens and twenties who had been trained by Hussein's secret service to conduct assassinations and suicide bombings. Brainwashed and erratic, the Fedayeen who were dispersed throughout the region exasperated US military endeavors.

On my first mission in tandem with the US military police, we targeted the house of Hussein's cousin, catching six Fedayeen by surprise. Trembling and stunned to silence by the attack, hatred seething through the sandbags covering their eyes, their young voices cracked as they reluctantly verbalized one-word answers to the questions I forcibly posed in Arabic. We piled our captives into a Humvee to transport them back to the base, and as we made a U-turn on the road, another Fedayeen launched an ambush attack.

Bullets pelted the Humvee as if it were made of plywood because we were not yet equipped with armored vehicles. Leaving the six Fedayeen tied up in the Humvee, we each hurtled into a ditch, nestling like sturdy clumps of weeds along the row of gorgeous red roses that lined the curb. Since I was an interpreter and not a soldier, I did not have body armor or a helmet and was all too aware that at any instant a bullet could jab through my ribs or a grenade could spark a fire in the rosebushes, setting me ablaze as well. As we lay there huddled along the road, deliberately separated from one another so that we would not become a collective target for our enemies, one of the soldiers sent a distress signal via radio. Soon, above the clatter of the bullet fire, I heard the churning blades of an Apache helicopter that swooped onto the scene, blistering the ambush with rapid fire, as if plucking the strings on an oud with quickened fervor that numbs the fingers of the player and numbs the senses of any person within earshot. Finally, the tune resolved. Rescued, we gathered the six captives who, remarkably, had remained strapped in the Humvee. They went to prison while I emerged from my first mission successful, my adrenaline surging and my mind grappling with the crucial part that I was playing in a war on my own turf.

About three months later, in the summer of 2003, I was assigned to the Iraqi police academy in Tikrit, this time under US leadership. Along with ninety-nine other Iraqis, I attended classes Monday through Friday from 8:00 a.m. to 2:00 p.m. The instruction was substantially more thorough than when I had studied at the Iraqi-run academy. I learned how to investigate crimes and how to draft case reports, interpreting the facts accurately so that the data could be presented to a judge.

They began to train our class of one hundred men to use guns, showing us how to handle a gun, how to protect it from being snatched by an adversary, and how to take a gun from someone else. Incrementally, they took us to the shooting range in groups of four or five to practice with mock wooden pistols. It was obvious that the US military police were reluctant to put guns in the hands of the Iraqis, lacking the missing ingredient of a relationship of trust. For all they knew, any of us might turn on them and stage a revolt. They told us that if we made any wrong move, we would instantly be shot, and we had to look directly at the target without glancing left or right. We were commanded to shoot all of the bullets at the target, place the gun down, put our hands up, and walk away from the firing stance. Fulfilling the strict expectations, I was selected to join them on missions, and my father was very proud of my progress, pleased that I was assisting the US soldiers in their campaign.

On my last mission with the US military police in the desert, we found a group of Iraqi men in an SUV loaded with boxes of mortar rounds and rocket launchers. They were equipped with manuals in Arabic that detailed the procedures for detonating and propelling explosives. I questioned them on behalf of the Americans, and the men told me that they were merely keeping the empty boxes to construct a beehive. One of the US soldiers was browsing through one of the munition user guides as I translated the false claim that the men were pursuing a honey-making business. Appalled at the ridiculousness of it all, he promptly slammed the book on the head of the culprit next to him. Arresting the men, we forced them to climb into the back of the SUV so that we could haul them and all of their equipment back to the police station.

I was appointed as the driver because US soldiers were not allowed to drive civilian vehicles. There was only one barrier—I had never driven a car at all, and it was a manual transmission SUV. As I sat poised behind the steering wheel, one of the US soldiers sat next to me, tutoring me through every gear shift. At one point, I swung too wide on a curve and almost rammed the SUV into a house. The more the SUV jerked along, the more the US soldiers were terrifically amused, telling others via radio about my escapade. When we eventually arrived at the station, they applauded exuberantly for my accomplishment as a novice driver. Finally, they were beginning to treat me like one of their own, exhibiting the trust that I knew I deserved.

As darkness fell at the end of that successful day, my elation evaporated in the dry desert night. That night we lost a soldier. Some Fedayeen approached the station gate in a Humvee loaded with a fifty kilogram machine gun so powerful that if a bullet were to graze past a man in thin air, it could ravage his face. One of their shots ripped off the jaw of a soldier, and another bullet landed squarely in a soldier's stomach. With one man down, the US military police arrested all of us Iraqi recruits, stripping us naked and examining our bodies for tattoos. Within hours of having sat behind the wheel of the SUV, amiably supporting the efforts of my American comrades, now I was a suspect. They were looking for any signs that I might be an inside traitor, any insignia that might brand me as a Fedayeen informer. They identified one of the new Iraqis as guilty of betraying his loyalty to the US military. Finding me innocent, with no incriminating tattoos, the US soldiers were genuinely relieved, hugging me apologetically.

Being scrutinized put a bad taste in my mouth, but I chose to dismiss my misgivings and continued to establish myself as a trustworthy collaborator alongside the US leadership. In our off-hours, I strove to grasp the nuances of American military English that I had never learned in school. I would scribble every new word on paper so that I could expand my vocabulary and communicate like one of the guys. They often spoke in code, spelling words in ways that became more familiar and less cryptic the longer I listened. If they started to say "Alpha Bravo Bravo," I knew they were talking about Abbas, although everyone called me Tex. For as long as I can remember, I used to tell people that my dream was to live in Texas, and that became my nickname. It was gratifying to hear the Americans gradually embrace me as Tex, a brother in arms.

I graduated from the US military police academy on August 28, 2003, and returned to the same police station in Tikrit, working once again alongside Iraqi compatriots. To my chagrin, my superiors immediately assigned me to be a physical interrogator, a euphemism for a position that required torturing captives in order to provoke a confession. They wanted me to torture a man whom they thought was a terrorist, and I declined, saying that I was not trained in torture tactics and did not want to perpetuate the abusive strategies that had reigned under Hussein's authority. My refusal to comply with the harsh expectations generated an alternative order: "Pack your bags."

I no longer had a position with the Iraqi police force. In their minds, I had quit. In my mind, I had held on to my conviction that torture was wrong. As I gathered my belongings in the dorm, my thoughts plummeting with the gravity of my terminated career, a fellow Iraqi police officer walked toward me between the rows of bunk beds. With hushed insistence, he spoke: "Colonel Assad was talking to other high-ranking officers about killing you," he confided. "He does not like that you are working so closely with the United States military." I had been labeled as a traitor. The officer urged me to leave at once and to be careful.

Heeding his cautionary imperative and tossing my personal items into a bag, I heard a fleet of Humvees pulling into the parking lot at the police station. Curious about this unexpected arrival, I stepped outside and saw several US Army officers and civilian private contractors. Inquisitive, I approached them to introduce myself as the only English-speaker nearby. My language abilities put them at ease, and they told me about their purpose in coming to the station. They were on a recruitment mission, the genesis of a SWAT team that was the brainchild of one of the US coalition colonels. His vision was to train Iraqi police officers to serve as SWAT team members for the US military. I hardly knew what that meant, but I was immediately intrigued.

"I would like to join the SWAT team," I told them, craving a new challenge. One detail stood in the way—I was no longer a police officer.

The SWAT recruiters were unable to enlist anyone outside of the Iraqi police force, so I called my father, determined to discover a path forward. He had been so supportive of my collaboration with the US military, and he would surely figure out a way to overcome this hurdle. As I had hoped, my father understood my quandary and my keen desire to be a SWAT member. Within minutes, he put down the phone and drove from Samarra to the police station in Tikrit. He stood by my side as I filled out paperwork to formally reenlist in the Iraqi police force. Although my qualifications on paper may have looked fine, the fact that I had been terminated that same day as a police officer seemed to soil my record beyond repair. With the utmost respect, my father spoke with a high-ranking Iraqi police officer, convincing him to accept me back into service.

After a day of upheaval where I had lost my rank but kept my conscience, I was once again a police officer. This time, I was on a track that I anticipated would steer clear of torture, contributing instead to introducing a new order of morality. I would be joining the first SWAT team in Iraq.

CHAPTER SEVEN

The US SWAT instructor approached me. "We are testing the cadets on their shooting skills with an AK-47," he said. "Come." I had never shot a full-fledged weapon before, only the wooden pistols during training classes at the police academy. I followed him, not wanting to admit my inexperience.

At the range, the recruitment appraisers placed in my hands an AK-47 and one thirty bullet magazine. The target was twenty-five feet away from me as I pointed my feet and straightened my shoulders, my posture feigning confidence. I pulled the trigger with resolve, each roaring detonation shaking my arms.

Not one bullet hit the target. Trying to disguise my shame, I looked at the SWAT instructor who was evaluating me and asserted, "There is something wrong with the gun."

Without saying a word, the man took the gun from me, inserted a magazine, loaded the chamber. Turning toward the target, he fired one shot. The bullet hit spot on. He looked at me, put his hand on my shoulder, and said, "SWAT stands for Special Weapons and Tactics." His voice was serious but kind, entertained. "You need to learn the tactics and know how to shoot."

My excitement collapsed, catching up with the reality that each of my bullets had fallen off the target and onto the ground. By all appearances, I lacked the caliber to join this special operations force. The instructor's next statement shocked me. "I can see that you want it," he said. "Go meet with the colonel at Saddam's birthday palace."

The next morning, April 1, 2004, I arrived at the improvised military base occupying Hussein's birthday palace in Tikrit. Before I even met the colonel, I was issued an inventory of gear: a uniform, kneepads, elbow pads, gloves, boots, a bullet-proof vest, plus textbooks on SWAT methodologies. The colonel greeted me with a handshake, saying, "Welcome," and appointed some of his guards to take me to the shooting range.

They taught me the techniques of shooting an AK-47, demonstrating how to aim, how to breathe. My accuracy improved dramatically, and they were surprised. Taking me back to their superiors, they affirmed, "He is good." After passing further physical, mental, and personality tests, I awaited their decision. I watched as other new Iraqi lieutenants came for examination as well, embarrassed and frustrated to observe their immaturity. This was war, not a game, and their antics to trick the US soldiers, even in jest, were repulsive to me. At the end of the week, the SWAT instructors read aloud the names of the individuals who had been selected to attend formal SWAT school.

"Abbas Hameed."

My emotions effervesced even as I maintained my cool military composure. I was in. I had become a legitimate member of the SWAT team. As the First Battle of Fallujah was raging that same week, targeting militants who had killed private US military contractors and soldiers, I was definitively choosing sides. I received a 9mm Glock 17 not only to use, but to keep. And soon I would be firing bullets from weapons even more powerful, aiming to be an agent of change for good in Iraq.

The very next day, Saturday, I started to attend SWAT school in Baghdad at a discreet location unknown to locals. In addition to the pistol, I was issued an AK-47 with buttstock, the tool of my new trade. Soon I would acquire the remaining standard gear, including a pouch containing a smoke grenade, a flashbang, a third grenade, and four magazines for my weapon—two on my left hip, one in my holster, one in my gun. The rigorous program lasted seventy-five days, seven days per week. Each day began at 5:00 a.m. By 6:30 a.m., we were already at the shooting range, staying there until 7:00 p.m., with only a quick forty-five-minute lunch at midday and a hurried dinner.

We deliberately practiced shooting at night, holding a gun in one hand and a light in the other, crisscrossing our arms and shifting positions rapidly so that our supposed enemy could not identify the exact location of the light source. We would also stage fake ambushes on our instructors as a learning exercise and gained concentrated skills in breaching buildings, spying, hostage situations, transporting valuable personnel, and interrogating. The US institutors of the SWAT regiment instilled in us principles of how to instruct the Iraqi police corps. The overall vision for the inaugural SWAT team was to sculpt a legitimate, long-term structure for the safety of Iraq. The training was intense, and I thrived. I especially liked the shooting drills where we would walk in formation and suddenly hear a trainer shouting an order to turn left or right and shoot.

After the first forty-five days, the instructors pulled me aside. They had noticed that my rudimentary skills as a shooter had soared, and I was excelling. No longer would I be a regular SWAT member—they decided to accelerate my training so that I could become a sniper. My self-esteem swelled, my career on target now that I knew how to stare intently down the barrel of a gun and obliterate the bull's-eye. Undoubtedly, I had tunnel vision, only aware of seeing my own world in this larger atmosphere where the nations were clashing upon the turf of my beloved Iraq. Collaborating with the US military was a personal achievement, and no longer was I floundering in the waters of the Tigris River, struggling to stay afloat. I was admittedly culpable of being cocky, proud of my accomplishments and feeling invincible. Death was not even a consideration.

The SWAT instructors redirected me to a specialized course focused on crafting me into a sniper. It was a fast month of watching tactical videos and then actively imitating the procedures, an overwhelming volume of material, and yet my urge to be a sniper did not waver. They issued me a standard-issue military sniper weapon, an M24 rifle, placing into my hands the mechanism by which I would be entrusted with quelling the perilous environment of Iraq.

But first, before graduating and being commissioned, I had to prove my competence in a demanding examination. For the final evaluation exercise, they paired me with a Shia classmate, a young man whose Muslim beliefs differed from my Sunni background but whose skill on the field was noteworthy, regardless of any religious distinctions. On the ground, religion meant nothing to us. Six SWAT officers scrutinized every move as we stood at attention in full gear, our torsos strong underneath our body armor, our backs straight despite the weight of our bulky backpacks, our shoulders steadily supporting our rifle cases. We had to run 250 feet with all of our gear, crawl back to the starting line, run the same distance again, and then return, crawling. Poised alongside the Shia man, I prepared to fire my rifle in the final test. Thinking quickly, I called out my choice on the target, opting for the nose because it was a larger triangular shape, while my examination partner aimed for the mouth. Simultaneously, the two of us had to shoot so precisely that it would sound like a single bullet. We counted out loud.

"1 . . . 2 . . .," I said, cutting myself off at 3 so that not one brief breath would cause my arms to quiver.

It was a perfect shot. One of the instructors kicked me playfully from behind, proud of my achievement. While the task ahead of me was serious, the comradery that I shared with men like him was a lifeline, as we genuinely watched each other's backs in battle and in life itself. Little did I know that I would need the guidance of a father figure more and more, on and off the field.

I had become an authorized sniper for the US military, ready to join the rest of the SWAT team, ready for action. The entire team went to Tikrit to receive orders from the US Army, which stirred up past recollections of my last stint at that location. Remaining at the Iraqi police station in Tikrit meant risking my life. I spoke quietly with my captain, revealing the dire news that Colonel Assad had told people to shoot me, accusing me of being a traitor who was too closely allied with the US military. I was sure that his vengeance would escalate now that I was a sniper. The captain listened and, with stern seriousness, stepped away to have a private conversation with one of his peers.

Momentarily, my captain returned and said, "You are going to be OK. You will be staying with us." He made arrangements to keep me under close watch at Hussein's birthday palace in Tikrit. I shared a room with two Iraqi senior interpreters, a safer location to launch my new career.

If the atmosphere surrounding Colonel Assad's threats was dangerous, perhaps even more alarming was knowing that I could never visit my own home in Samarra again. My father advised me that one of our relatives was expressing extreme distaste for my collaboration with the US military, telling neighbors near our shared property that he intended to put an unnamed traitor into the trunk of his car. It was obvious that I was his target, the traitor he wanted to eliminate. A sniper is meant to hit targets, not be a target himself, and my father was concerned, recommending that I should go to the US as soon as I had the opportunity. He planned to tell people that I had been blasted by an Improvised Explosive Device (IED), with no trace left of my body. From this point onward, I never returned to Samarra, never felt the embrace of my extended family. Instead, my arms were grasping a weapon on behalf of another nation, becoming an enemy of my own land. Being rejected by fellow Iraqis angered me enough to consider taking revenge, but I knew that the wiser path was to take refuge in the protection of the US military, supporting their efforts to establish an environment of peace.

CHAPTER EIGHT

A M24 rifle and a Dragon Elf Iraqi rifle were my loyal companions as a sniper, as well as an AK-47, which I used primarily on raids. My first of ten lone sniper missions was to target IEDs along the Main Supply Route Tampa, an expansive highway that runs north to south. To the untrained eye, it appeared to be a vast, sand-swept route flanked by nothing but desert, while it was furtively embedded with fiery explosives. The incendiary capacity under the sizzling sand prompted soldiers to call it "Highway to Hell."

Following a lead conveyed by my SWAT teammates, I positioned myself on top of a newly built two-story building overlooking the highway, my eyes on alert for anyone with a subversive scheme. At thirty minutes past midnight, long after the 10:00 p.m. curfew, the horizon should have been empty except for the moths and other flying insects shimmying in the beams of light cast by lamps along the highway. With a direct sight line to the roadside from about one quarter mile away, I easily spotted a man carrying a 155mm artillery round, quite cumbersome, about two feet long. Walking surreptitiously in the darkness, his frame and the bulky IED in his arms seemed to blink under my watchful stare. This was no pedestrian. My duty prompted calculated action.

My purpose as a sniper was straightforward—shoot to wound, not to kill. Calling my captain, I notified him about the sighting, and he authorized me to do whatever was necessary. That did not mean the freedom to be trigger-happy. It was against protocol to fire a shot if the man was only carrying the IED, so I held my gaze and my gun steadily. I observed each nimble movement of this cunning wildcat, his furtive feline eyes oblivious that his predator was watching as he placed the IED on the surface of the road. That was my cue. I promptly focused, my finger on the smooth trigger. In less than a breath, I squeezed and took a shot, aiming for the man's thigh. The bullet lacerated his knee, and he toppled, wailing so loudly that I could hear every mounting moan.

"Target down," I declared via radio. A division of my SWAT unit came from two miles away to apprehend the terrorist, while someone else came to pick me up. My first mission accomplished, adrenaline pulsing, I returned to the base, poised in a constant state of readiness. Not every assignment was a solo sniper mission like those ten appointments directed toward IED emplacers as well as members of Hussein's internal security force. Other days were filled with capturing high-value targets, which we understood to be terrorists, joining the US Army to conduct raids, or escorting private US contractors back to their home base.

A few weeks later, I accompanied other SWAT team members who were ordered to escort a high-value officer in the Iraqi Army from Tikrit to Baiji, an industrial city about fifty minutes north. I was appointed as the gunner, wielding a PKC machine gun as a precaution to ensure the safety of our passenger. After taking Captain Jabar Nazar to his home, we cruised back toward our base, retracing our route on the only road linking the two cities, the tar-like darkness engulfing our convoy as we drove purposefully, our ears on alert in the hushed night.

Abruptly, an ambush spattered the smooth landscape, machine guns expelling bullets that cracked the veil of night and enveloped our vehicles. Ducking at every blast, I scanned the unfamiliar terrain through my night vision goggles and quickly spotted the tracer rounds of the attackers. I could see that the bullets were coming from clumps of tall grasses and bushes, so I pointed my PKC in that direction and sprayed the area with rapid fire. The perpetual sound was like a pounding drumbeat, like the traditional percussion instruments of Iraq, but accelerating into a frenzy that was anything but festive. After fifteen harrowing minutes of nonstop combat, all was quiet. The only next sound was the undaunted shout from a convoy member, confirming that he had survived the assault, and the others echoed their agreement. Intact, we sped onward to Tikrit, reporting the incident to our captain and recognizing once again the perils of every expedition, even an unfussy road trip, in the dark panorama of wartime.

At times, we became engaged with activities to protect the livelihood of local citizens who were encountering these same perils. While the status-based missions to target terrorists were our overt focus, alongside our commitment to provide security for high-ranking officers, we balanced these priorities with an attentive posture toward the people of Iraq. One of these individuals was an Iraqi janitor who labored faithfully at the US Army base. A young father in his thirties, he was softhearted and service-oriented, always cleaning the facility beyond the expectations of his role, always smiling. Often, he would gather pieces of garbage next to us at the table which we would have willingly discarded ourselves, his diligence unmatched. One day, he was oddly quiet, his lips pursed, his eyes downcast. SWAT training had taught us to be attuned to any unique variables, averting ploys before they could be consummated and remaining sensitive to environmental signals that seemed offbeat.

The other men on the team prodded me, saying, "Tex, ask him."

I approached the janitor, still perplexed that he was in no mood to exchange smiles. Instead, tears welled up in his eyes as I greeted him, my tone careful to keep him at ease. Swallowing the lump in his throat, he began to divulge the reason for his downhearted demeanor. A neighbor was threatening to kidnap and kill his wife and twin four year-old daughters as a fierce retaliation for his affiliation with the US military, the infidel. As a janitor, he exerted his energy to earn wages for the rental house that he shared with his precious family.

"If I quit, my family will be hungry," he told me in anguish, the reality of the threat hitting him hard. We both knew that he had to be extremely cautious, given the raging climate of Iraq. As our policy dictated, we decided not to take formal action in case his neighbor was merely bluffing. The janitor chose to keep working.

Three days later, the janitor sprinted back to the base after his lunch break, breathless because of the stifling news he was carrying. I was not there when he arrived but was summoned as the prime candidate to discover what was so wrong. Besides being a sniper, I was also an interpreter, medic, and interrogator, so I went with my SWAT unit to the base. As soon as I got close, I could see that the janitor was hysterical. Through his sobs, he poured out his story.

The janitor had gone home for lunch, and instead of a warm, spicy meal of leftover eggplant stew prepared by his sweet wife, he found the front door open, the house trashed. The carpet in the main living space was crooked and rumpled, chairs upended, pillows strewn. More upsetting than anything was the flagrant quiet—his wife did not greet him from the kitchen, and his daughters were not giggling down the hallway. Instantaneously, he knew that they had been kidnapped.

I asked him the name of the menacing neighbor, gathering other SWAT members to go conduct a search. Not finding any further clues at the janitor's house, we inquired at the nearby houses, looking for the suspected kidnapper, and learned that the neighbor owned another house. No one knew exactly where the second house was, or what had happened to the problematic neighbor and his two sons. As we heard this, we located the neighbor's younger son, a twelve year-old boy, constraining him to go with us even though he was silent, scared, shivering. He refused to talk.

Putting a sandbag over the boy's head, I ushered him to the

SWAT vehicle, then promptly removed the sandbag. Trying to intimidate him with words rather than by physical force, I said, "If you do not tell me where your father and your older brother are, you will go to jail for them and never see them again."

As the boy struggled to maintain his statuesque pose, his posture became more defiant. Leaning toward him, I added, "You would probably die in prison."

At this, he spat out the words, "My father is across the Tigris River at his farmhouse." Our team departed immediately, following the boy's hesitant directions and finding an obscure house tucked in the middle of a farm. We surrounded the house and barged into the living room, where clear plastic film used for greenhouses was spread across the floor, creating a ghastly staging area. Cameras were already set in position, aimed toward a large Allahu Akbar sign proclaiming that Allah is the greatest, the beautiful calligraphy defiled by its foreboding message. The evidence glared at us, a warning that within moments this would become the scene of a gruesome torture. Soon, they would be beheading their victims and recording the episode in order to incite further fear.

For us, there was no time to waste, and for the kidnapper there was also no time to escape. He was there in the farmhouse, along with his older son, and we took them into custody, then searched quickly for the captives. In a separate shed, surrounded by confused goats, we found the janitor's wife and twin daughters lying on the dirty floor, their legs and wrists bound with ropes. The little girls whimpered as their mother tried to comfort them, her face pale with apprehension, her chest trembling.

With words as firm and kind as possible, not wanting to aggravate her anxiety, we told her that we were SWAT members. "We will take you and your daughters back to your house, back to your husband," we said. "First, we want to be sure that you are not injured." Gently removing the ropes, we took the fragile trio to a US military hospital to be examined. When they were released with no injuries, only some sore bruises, we were relieved, escorting them back to the welcoming arms of the irreproachable young man who had been our janitor. We wanted to keep him near to us, not only because of his impeccably clean performance around the military base but also because we now wished we could keep him safe forever. However, we advised him to consider leaving for the sake of insulating his family from further intimidation. And we knew that we had done our part, locking up the kidnapper and his eighteen year-old son for ten years.

Starting in October 2004, I was assigned to ensure the personal protection of two private US contractors in both mobile and static operations training. I highly respected these men, and it was a privilege to be responsible for their safety. Not everyone held the same posture of dependability, and I was irritated to observe some of the new Iraqi SWAT lieutenants joking about the American soldiers. The lieutenants were green and immature, thinking that playing pranks was part of the game of wartime. Then they took their tricks to the extreme.

When I heard them bragging about plotting to use guns as part of their trickery, I turned to one of the Iraqi lieutenants and said, "If you shoot a bullet, I will shoot you." That was enough to quell his levity.

Soon after that, I overheard another one of the fresh recruits whispering about ambushing one of the private contractors under my guard. "If you hurt him, I will hurt you," I told the lawless lieutenant. I also alerted the contractor to what we both hoped was harmless bravado, and the gossip seemed to settle.

However, the lull was short-lived. I was escorting the two private contractors back to their home base when a car up ahead stopped, causing a traffic jam in the streets of Tikrit. Always scanning the horizon, I spotted a man perched high on a building one hundred yards away, his lurking figure protruding out of place against the sultry sky. I exited the vehicle to peer at the roadblock and assess the route, my eyes keenly aware of the man whose stance seemed unusual. One of the contractors started to get out too, curious to see what was causing the snarled traffic and blaring horns.

Standing on the blistering pavement, I heard an Arabic voice I recognized, one of the new lieutenants, saying, "Hey, let those pigs come out. We have other guys who are going to shoot at them."

Urgently, I ordered the contractor next to me to get back inside the vehicle, raising my voice to my superior in a life-and-death situation where proper military protocols mattered less than preserving life. He promptly heeded my command, clambering out of view. The foreign contractor had just barely latched the door when bullets started flying as a man stepped around a corner, aiming a rifle. I watched every slinking move of the man whose rifle gawked at me, and as he fired one round, I fired back to disturb his ugly fervor. Startled by my unhesitating retaliation, the shooter ran away. Upon investigation, we learned that he was a friend of one of the SWAT lieutenants who had stolen a sniper rifle to ambush the US contractors. No one was injured, the lieutenant was terminated, and I was satisfied that I had successfully fulfilled my assignment.

My pride was always in a job well done, a service to the mission of the US military. No one had been hurt in this incident, and that was the best result I could desire. It never made me proud to kill another man, nor did I keep a tally, unlike others who counted their morbid triumphs. A sniper is a shooter, yes, but also a disciplined man on a mission. I was taught to be assertive, but I was whacked during training if I kept my finger on the trigger of the gun. Keeping my mind clear in the midst of chaos, I could only touch the trigger if I saw that my target was intent on harming me. If the tumult turned bloody, I still knew that the individual at the other end of the barrel was a human being. As I often told the US soldiers, "Do not make it your own. Leave it behind." And so, I moved from one mission to the next, never on a death hunt and never wanting to think about death much at all—including mine.

CHAPTER NINE

The stakes were high in the global sphere, where a single spark could ignite weapons of mass destruction, where a single bullet from a sniper's rifle could extinguish the perpetration of ruinous evil. In the late spring of 2005, I participated in a recon, gathering information about a high-level Iraqi individual of interest, a man whose status in Saddam Hussein's government made him notorious. His villainous reputation had long attracted the attention of the international community, and the US Defense Intelligence Agency was concerned about the continuation of his heinous acts. I was surprised to unearth evidence that he was still residing in the country, because the rumor was that he had devised a getaway. Once we had completed the recon phase, my SWAT captain appointed me to conduct a solo sniper mission targeting this loathsome leader. Shocked that they trusted me rather than selecting a US soldier for such a pivotal assignment, I recognized the gravity of my responsibilities. A bombastic powerhouse was difficult enough to encounter, and even more when his threats could easily materialize into widespread carnage. My solid training and staunch rifle could be decisive.

Reconnaissance data indicated that the militant leader would be arriving at a hospital in Tikrit at 2:00 a.m., unsuspecting that his habitual blood work appointments had been detected by US surveillance. We developed a detailed stratagem, and I tucked a map of the access routes and firing angles into the pocket of my black SWAT uniform, a nighttime camouflage disguise to blend into the darkness, covering the upsurge of adrenaline speeding through my sinews. The inconspicuous pitch-dark SUV shuttling me to the location slowed down as it approached a complex and then crawled in front of a building near the hospital so that I could jump out on the run.

I snuck into the building, climbing four flights of stairs to reach the roof level. Squatting in one corner of the flat roof under the clear midnight sky, unwavering in the almost unnoticeable hot breeze, using my legs as a natural tripod for my rifle, I peered through night vision goggles toward the hospital. A trusted accessory, the goggles made me feel like a solitary, farsighted owl, penetrating the sunless distance with binocular accuracy. The eighteen inch wall along the edge of the roof was the perfect height to rest the tip of the gun's barrel, and I propped it on a pair of socks filled with beans for stability. I knew that the individual would be entering the hospital through a door in the back, about one mile away, a prearranged privilege for his high-profile status, and that he would exit through another door, only about a half-mile from where I crouched. My 180-degree sight line offered a direct view of the hospital exit, with nothing littering the path for the bullet that I would shoot.

In the stillness, I heard footsteps coming from somewhere inside the building beneath me. Someone was in the stairwell, each thump of his shoe louder than the previous one. The roof access door opened, and I dropped to the floor, curling my dark-clad shape into a dot so that no one could see my leggy spider-like position nor my rifle. A civilian man wearing a white dishdasha walked slowly to the corner farthest from me, using a cigarette lighter as a flashlight. His catlike prowl disclosed the intentions of a man on the hunt. Apparently, he had heard something and wanted to detect the source of the sound. He retraced his steps back to the middle of the building and then cantered to the other corner, his wary arm extending left and right with the flickering lighter. I was poised to kill him if he walked toward me, but he never once approached the corner where I huddled. Then, just as unannounced as when he arrived, he left.

Even with the trespasser gone, I could no longer proceed because the entire mission had lost its secrecy. It was very likely that the civilian was picking up on some cue when he patrolled the roof, even if his equipment seemed so amateur. I called headquarters, advising them that someone had been on the roof but that they had not seen me. The voice on the other end of the line said, "Your backup will arrive and pick you up," declaring that the mission had failed. Still on alert, I stretched my limbs and returned to the stairwell, holding my pistol ready for any attack as I descended to the ground floor. When my backup team came, they deliberately made a lot of noise in the building, wanting to assert our presence. People knew not to pick a fight with the SWAT force because we had a reputation for not tolerating the status quo of Iraq.

"What happened?" I asked my captain when I returned to the base. He told me that there had been a leak. The SWAT authorities identified the culprit, someone within the Joint Command Center, and released him from his duties without charges. The failure of the mission was a defeat, for sure, and yet at a personal level I had not lost my life. If the civilian scouring the roof had sauntered to the fourth corner, if he had pulled a weapon from underneath the folds of his flowing dishdasha, I could have become his prey. Instead, I had walked down those four flights of stairs with an unfired bullet and a fire within me to face the dynamite of another day.

It was 3:00 a.m. when I finally went to the barracks, not really ready to relax and yet exhausted after the strain of the sniper mission. Trying not to keep the other five men awake, I lay still on my top bunk, but my brain was spinning. The days of sloshing through the meadowlands of the Tigris River with my brother, even the day when I had almost drowned, seemed like a blissful, distant memory. I held no gun back then, nor did I hold the responsibility of attempting to reverse the downward spiral of Iraq's governance.

Now I was a sniper, tasked with aiming my gun at power-hungry, malignant men, exposing myself to an evil environment where any day I could be the target instead of the shooter, the prey instead of the hunter. Everlasting peace was an accomplishment beyond my grasp. And yet, I thrived on the challenge, thrilled to be at the crux of the action. Finally, after an hour, my thoughts stopped their groggy pirouettes, dropping into a deep sleep.

The dynamite of another day began with an explosion at 6:00 a.m., startling me from what had been nothing more than a nap after the previous night's exertion. I sprang out of my bunk along with the other men. An abrupt rumble shook the barracks with such a roar that we thought it was an earthquake, and our radios started going crazy with chatter. We ran outside with our gear, reporting immediately to the captain.

Still receiving the breaking news, our captain informed us that terrorists had denotated a car bomb outside the gate of the Iraqi police academy in Tikrit. US soldiers were already on the scene, and he ordered us to join them, to be on the lookout for a secondary bomb. We knew that the typical terrorist tactic was twofold—a first bomb to attract attention and draw a gathering of people, followed by a second bomb to cause more damage. Driving 90 to 100 mph, we arrived outside the police academy and asked the US lieutenant in charge what he wanted us to do. He appointed us to an area that was not covered by military personnel, placing an Iraqi sniper on a house overlooking an empty lot littered with construction debris. This sniper was the same Shia man who had been tested with me in sniper training, whose sharp eyes were dimmed by the weariness that our incessant schedule imposed. His drowsiness muffled his capacity, and his presence was ultimately inconsequential that morning, even as the sun started to rise. It was June 13, the temperatures pleasantly balanced and comfortable for any of us in uniform before the heat of midday— so comfortable that the Shia sniper succumbed to his sleepiness as he lay on top of the house.

Meanwhile, as other SWAT men were scattered in various positions about one hundred feet away in each direction, I was on foot on the ground, near a cluster of houses not far from the police academy. It was a two-way street, with one lane on each side of a raised median dotted with light poles and palm trees. There was no traffic, only two parked cars, one on each side of the divided street. I walked toward the gravel road leading to the construction dump site, watching for any unusual movement, then came back to inspect the parked cars for anything suspicious. All was calm, the tension limited to my own sensation that at any instant a dreaded second bomb might convulse, kindling a furiously black cloud that would shield the sun as it absentmindedly cheered the eastern horizon.

Turning from one of the empty parked cars, I noticed five Iraqi police officers standing uneasily on the median, one of them restlessly leaning against a light pole. Unarmed, they were more a loitering hazard than a help. I approached them to recommend that they leave, since the threat of a flare-up still hovered in the cool morning air. They rejected my admonition, preferring to linger and verify if their friends at the police academy had safely escaped the earlier bomb. Again, I tried to assure them that their buddies were fine, but they insisted, despite my warnings.

"We will stay," one of the Iraqi police officers contended.

"Suit yourself," I said, stepping away as I heard a car approaching, its tires gnawing at the gravel on the side road.

Looking toward the sound, I saw the front of a pale green station wagon as it pulled off the gravel onto the pavement of the street where I stood in front of the police academy. As it cruised toward me, I raised my left hand, signaling the driver to stop. When it continued to advance, I clenched my left hand into a fist while raising my rifle in my right hand, forming an X with my arms, an alternative command to stop. Not knowing the nationality of the driver and his interpretation of my motions, I swiftly experimented with several stop gestures to impel him to hit the brakes. Instead, he began to speed toward me.

The front end of the station wagon was tilted upward, the back end dragging lower under the weight of a load that the suspension was never intended to haul. I made direct eye contact with the driver. There was a sleazy steadfastness in his look, his eyes portending the finality of his purpose. Apart from his cumbersome cargo, he was alone in the vehicle, his long raven hair slicked back with gel, his locked jaw green from a one-day shave, his hand clenched on the wheel with ferocity. I stood still, watching with wide-awake willpower. When his speed brought him a mere fifteen feet away from my feet, I aimed, pulled the trigger, and fired my rifle at his chest. At the sound and impact of a bullet with no return, he slumped, detonating a bomb in a loud, deafening explosion, the last achievement of a terrorist's final breath. A dozen 155mm artillery projectiles exploded in front of me in a plume of flames and smoke, and I flew into the air, defenseless against the immense pressure of the blast.

As gravity overtook the propulsion of the bomb, my airborne body slammed onto the asphalt, and I crawled to the curb, where there was a short wall grounding a metal fence. Aligning my body with the curb, I wished it were taller to shield me from the scorching fragments of shrapnel that spewed from the sky, remnants of the car that had sunk into a hole carved into the pavement by the cruel explosion. Stones and pebbles cluttered the atmosphere, as did the bullets that well-meaning but desperately irrational US soldiers started shooting at random angles. I felt the projectiles zipping past me, immobilized not by the bomb but by the reality that their disorderly friendly fire could hit me by accident. Something thudded on my back, like a dead weight, but I did not know what it was, nor did I dare to move. One of my SWAT colleagues sprinted down the street in the opposite direction, chased wildly by the raging car engine that was propelled by the heated burst, and losing a thumb to a renegade piece of shrapnel.

Each agonizing second was suspended above my prostrate

form as bullets and shrapnel rained down from a cloudless sky. Finally, I faintly heard the lieutenant bellow, "Cease fire! Cease fire!" The overzealous soldiers stopped shooting.

Only then did I allow myself to take inventory of my own vital signs. I feared the worst, wondering which limbs I may have lost, which internal organs may have imploded. I wondered if I was still able to be a man in every sense. A car bomb of that caliber should have killed me, but I was completely intact. No part of me was missing. Although my gloves had peeled away and the flesh on my hands felt scalding hot, my skin was not burned. The only visible evidence that I had just survived a horrific car bomb was a bruise on my knee, a sore spot from tumbling to the earth after catapulting toward heaven and back.

Astounded by the sheer sensation of being alive, of feeling oxygen inundating my lungs just like it always had, I started to get up from my refuge near the curb. As I did, the weight that had thumped onto my back glared at me grotesquely from the sidewalk, and I realized that it was a leg. I had been hit by a bloody bone, from the femur down to the foot, its straight, rigid structure disfigured by dangling scraps of meaty flesh. It was the detached leg of the bomber who had defiantly exchanged looks with me only a minute or two previously in the now distant past. Rather than stare with disgust, I clambered to my feet, grabbed my rifle that lay on the road, and ran the length of the short wall where I had landed. Turning back at the corner, I took a knee and pointed toward the spot where I had just been.

The lieutenant approached behind me and put his hand on my shoulder. Reacting, I turned to almost shoot him but refrained when I saw who it was. "It is OK," he said. I stood down. We remained on alert for another twenty minutes, determined that no third attack would infiltrate and offend our scrutiny.

The street was calm, too calm. There were no more attacks, only ashen silence as I surveyed the disaster. The bodies of the five Iraqi police officers lay strewn across the pavement, a repulsive reminder of their contention that they would stay on the scene, rejecting my recommendation. Their flesh was burned, ravaged into segments.

Seeing this prompted me to look at myself again in amazement, while a pounding headache prodded me to recognize the severity of an explosion that had enough pressure to disintegrate my whole being. My ears rang, but my heart had not skipped a single beat. Wincing from a slight twinge in the back of my right leg, I concluded that my rifle had struck against it when I had flown into the air. As I reached for my pistol, my fingers touched something that felt like tapioca pudding sliding down my holster and my pants. It was white, it was viscous, it was grey matter from the brain of the terrorist whose mind had conspired a stunt more macabre than he had imagined.

My mind disoriented but unimpaired, I walked back to the place where I had been lying, looking for my radio. The black pavement was scorched, blacker than black, peppered with wreckage. A distinct spot near the curb was clear, a space as long as the distance from my head to my feet, a fathomless open-air shelter in the warzone. The angelic imprint on the ground left an indelible mark on my mind.

Another soldier found my radio about thirty feet away. It was dead, just like so much else everywhere around me. The prevailing stench was a sickening mixture of burned flesh and fuel, charred synthetic fabrics on the victims and smoldering upholstery wafting from the place where the station wagon had sunk into the earth. I rallied with other military personnel to remove the corpses of the Iraqi police officers and to take several injured civilians to the hospital in a few Humvees, a pickup truck, and an SUV. There were about fifteen bodies in total, and I went along in the ramshackle caravan of vehicles since the lieutenant wanted me to be examined by a doctor.

In the commotion at the hospital, where victims gasped and moaned, I was the misfit, strangely poised, still holding my rifle as

I stood to the side waiting for my turn. An eclipsing peace spread over me like a soothing cloud muting the sizzling desert sun, as if the uproar spinning around me were a whole world apart. It was not a lightheaded sensation of nearly drowning, like that morbidly sunny day at the Tigris River when I was disarmed and flailing. Instead, serenity gripped my spirit, and I knew that the God who had saved my life was the Creator of heaven and earth.

I did not have time to stop and grapple with those thoughts, because the doctor stepped toward me to inquire about my injuries. There was nothing for him to see. His evaluation of my condition was cursory since I had no symptoms that warranted his attention. He peered into my ears, spied into my mouth, and decided that I was fine, not pausing to check my lungs or order any x-rays.

"Go," the doctor said, disinterested in me, his able-bodied patient, as he pulled the diaphragm piece of his stethoscope away from my chest after sensing my strong heart. As unconcerned as he was about my status, the chaos around us was a riotous racket. Relatives of the victims were beginning to arrive, their wails of grief resounding through the stern surfaces of the hospital corridor.

As I heeded his dismissive imperative and turned to leave, a voice in my spirit spoke one word, "Jesus," a thought that had nothing to do with the doctor or the mourners. The word seemed to come out of nowhere, and yet it penetrated the spiritual fog of this sad setting, where every sobbing relative bent over with grief was like a sheep bleating desperately for guidance and comfort.

Jesus was a name I did not know personally. I was born a Muslim, like any citizen of my country, which for me meant little more than a statement on my Iraqi birth certificate. My visits to the mosque in Samarra as a child had not exposed me to the true identity of the prophet Jesus, nor had my Catholic father ever told me much about the Son of God born to the Virgin Mary. Our household acknowledged that he had existed, and I was no stranger to the artwork of centuries past that depicted him as a precious baby.

But that was all. And yet, in this moment, the name of Jesus inundated me with the conviction that the God of the universe had covered me with his hand, preserving my life in the brutal pressure of the blast from the car bomb. This kind of care had not come from the God of Islam—this was the touch of my Creator, the touch of Jesus. Knowing nothing else, I was eager to begin searching.

But I was subject to other commands, other priorities, as a SWAT man in a wartime environment where existential quests were not the order of the day. Still stunned that I was alive, I relished being recognized by the US military as a hero. I had stood my ground, firing a decisive bullet at the chest of the Iraqi opposition, a terrorist whose bomb was an offense to everything that the SWAT mission represented. Instantly, the US soldiers respected me, and my reputation soared beyond the status of a mere local Iraqi man who was aiding their cause. I was on the side of the US, my well-trained, measured actions serving as proof.

With that, my reputation plummeted among my fellow Muslims. I had killed a Muslim man, an unforgivable transgression, regardless of the fact that he was hell-bent on a destructive course. As they resented me, I also resented them. To them, I was a traitor. To me, each of these embittered Muslims was an accomplice in the mess that Iraq had become. Simultaneously, rampant depravity lurked throughout the land like the wild boars of the Iraqi fields, plotting to devour anyone who wore a foreign uniform. As an Iraqi SWAT sniper with a bold stars-and-stripes badge on my shoulder, I had crossed the line, becoming a friend of Iraq's enemy. Everywhere I looked, there was a corruption of the ideals that I was seeking to uphold, wielding my gun as a sniper in defense of justice and peace. Our entire SWAT team was under verbal fire, accused of undermining the deceptive schemes of governmental structures at all levels. Corrupt, hidden values were more bellicose than the pronounced weapons of war, hampering our ability to proceed.

Within days, my superiors announced that they saw no other route than to dissolve the SWAT force completely, concluding the contract abruptly and pivoting in order to avoid worse consequences at the hands of the government. Losing this local battle in Tikrit was worth it if it preserved the larger goals at stake, and the US did not want to get embroiled in petty infighting. Stripped of my SWAT gear through no fault of my own, I was aimless. I could not return to Samarra due to the high risk of being targeted as a traitor trying to sneak back onto my home turf, nor did I want to work alongside the Iraqi police. I had seen too much of the disarray within those ranks and did not want to be associated with any unit that was promoting violence.

Resolved that I had no choice but to maintain my alliance with the US military operation, I spoke to my captain, suggesting that I could serve as an interpreter. He did not have to be convinced, understanding fully why I did not want to revert to my Iraqi police officer duties. He agreed that working as an interpreter seemed to be a viable alternative.

"I will keep you here for a week and spread the word," the US captain said. In the meantime, he assigned me to assist as an interpreter patrolling the gate at the Joint Command Center, located at Saddam Hussein's birthday palace in Tikrit, eight miles north of Auja, the village where he was born. Although by now it was the summer of 2005, eighteen months after Hussein was captured, the palace was traditionally the site of his birthday celebrations. Throughout his rule, Hussein returned every year with a robust military entourage for a lavish party with dozens of clan members. One-half mile away from the palace, the gate was a colossal structure straddling a two-way road, capped by an octagonal edifice and a glistening dome, an exquisite replica of the Dome of the Rock in Jerusalem. There were two checkpoints at the gate, the first manned by the Iraqi Army. I was appointed to the second checkpoint, operated by the US Army. It seemed to be a good interim post while I waited for further orders.

Seven days later, before the week was over, a car bomb exploded at the first entrance. Fragments of skin from the scalp of the suicide bomber, still attached to clumps of hair, catapulted to my post at the second checkpoint. I was uninjured, and yet the incident rattled my heart and mind, prompting me to wonder if a mysterious someone was chasing after me. Having just survived a treacherous attack the previous week, I started to feel doomed.

"I need to get out of here," I told my captain, attempting to mask my distress with an unflinching facade. Working too close to the Iraqis at the first checkpoint meant rubbing shoulders with unreliable men, and I had no tolerance for their maneuvers. I requested permission to transfer to another base where I could collaborate more with the US military and employ my skills as an interpreter, far from the constant friction with the Iraqis at the gate in Tikrit.

He agreed. "I will make an urgent call," he said. "Gather your things."

Among my basic belongings was a new pistol, a replacement for the one that had been plastered with the remnant of the bomber's brain. I had earned the pistol under such excruciating circumstances that it certainly was no prize, only a reminder that I was indeed still alive. Before I left, I gave two sets of my uniform to an Asian man who provided security to one of the US colonels, a gesture of the connection that we had developed in the service of a multinational purpose. He had always raved about my cool uniform, and I was proud to share my swagger with a man who was genuine.

However, I knew that another prized piece of equipment was not mine to take or give away—the night vision goggles that had empowered me as a sniper. They were a precious possession. With those goggles, I could sneak up on a target, I could approach the insurgency head-on, I could accomplish my mission. No one had marked in a book that the goggles were on loan to me, but they were not my property. My mother had taught me not to steal, a lesson that mattered to the man I had become, a trustworthy Iraqi in the service of a nation I admired. Upon exiting, when I relinquished the goggles, the US soldiers responded with respect, knowing that I had willfully returned a valuable accessory.

As I left behind the rifles, the tangible tools of a sniper, taking only the new pistol in my holster, I kept close to my chest the skills that I had acquired. Not only could I hold a gun, like in the first days of training as a police officer, but also shoot it with acumen, precision, and discipline. I had learned to look at Iraq from the muzzle of a rifle, putting my life at risk in the face of mass destruction. And I had learned that while the intimidation of the enemy was real, I was alive for a better reason. I still did not know exactly what that reason was, but I wanted to pursue it.

With a renewed sense of purpose and a determination to defy danger, I was ready. My posture of expectancy was soon met when one of the US captains approached me with formality. "Abbas," he began. Internally, I stood up straight, unaccustomed to hearing anything other than my nickname. Everyone called me Tex, even my superiors. What sort of marching orders were on the tip of his tongue?

"You are going to be working for the US military," he said, his manner becoming more at ease as he spoke. "Do not worry about this nonsense." And then I knew that the anticlimactic end of my SWAT career was only another beginning. This farewell to the garb and gear of a sniper was a plot twist guiding me forward to a new horizon in this battle where a truce was far out of view.

PHOTOS

Helping a farmer whose lambs got loose

Dehydrated during Operation Arrowhead Ripper, I needed an IV with fluids

Bradley armored vehicle transferring us to another location during Operation Arrowhead Ripper

Checkpoint—searching for bombs and weapons in vehicles

Saddam Hussein's birthday palace, which the US Army was using as a command center

Soldier dropped off for a mission at night

Abbas flexing his muscles

Malwiya Mosque in Samarra, Iraq, was used for sniper missions

Abbas prepared for a mission

SWAT school training, Abbas is on the far right

SWAT school training, practicing an ambush

SWAT school training, practicing shooting weapons/ live fire

Soldiers from the Eighty-Second Airborne

We found a source of water in the middle of the desert

Greeting a local kid—soldiers would bring candy to the kids to gain their trust

Greeting a group of local kids

Before a mission

Humvees securing perimeter while on a mission

Operation Swarmer, loading soldiers in helicopters

Operation Swarmer

Abbas posing for a photo during a break

CHAPTER TEN

Within an hour, a US lieutenant transported me to Forward Operating Base (FOB) Remagen Base in southern Tikrit. Formerly known as FOB Packhorse, it had been renamed Remagen the previous year after the first soldier killed in that area. I was assigned to the Third Infantry Division 2-7th as an interpreter to support the endeavors of the US military in a location that the Iraqi Air Force had administered before Operation Iraqi Freedom altered the landscape in 2003. I was ready to take my turn in this enterprise and be an agent for the good of the mission, for the good of my country.

The same lieutenant who had driven me to the base selected me to be his primary interpreter, and we formed a strong partnership. He relied heavily on my Arabic fluency, while I was grateful that he treated me with a spirit of comradery and sought to employ my skills to the maximum. To him, I was not merely a bilingual Iraqi; I was a man whose life deserved protection. As we traveled across precarious terrain in a Humvee, he insisted that I not sit in the normal seat of an interpreter, on the right side of the vehicle, directly above the gas tank. He knew that terrorists were likely to target that spot, and he always found a different place in the Humvee where I could sit.

Observing that I was not attached to my cell phone like so many of the other Iraqis, the lieutenant would often playfully nag me to call my family and assure my mother that all was well. I would brush off his suggestion amiably. Instead, I was focused on the task at hand, and I had an additional motive for not using my phone. I knew that if an IED were ever to explode in our vicinity while I was speaking in Arabic with family or friends, I could be considered a suspect. The US soldiers would naturally wonder if I had been plotting and giving signals in a language they could not understand. When the US personnel attempted to speak to me in their elementary Arabic, I would always answer them in English. As a result, they trusted me increasingly, assured that I was one of them by choice, not a devious mercenary. I had nothing to hide.

Working as an interpreter was not my only duty when I was based at Remagen. In collaboration with the lieutenant, I also helped the team to conduct sniper missions, went on raids, interrogated terrorists, and visited mosques to gather information. We would park outside a mosque so that I could listen to what the imam was saying, trying to discern if he was inciting the population to fight against the infidels or take revenge against the US If I heard any condemnatory words, after the crowd dispersed from the mosque, we would grab the imam, zip-tie his wrists, and put him in a vehicle for further interrogation.

Interrogating any suspect was serious business, and I worked diligently to perfect the art of extracting information from men whose lips were sealed. The intelligence office would say, "Hey, Tex, we have a guy who is a big target," summoning me to pump details out of the depths of his brain.

The office would provide tea and a single cigarette as a ploy to loosen the man's resolve, but I refused to use those amenities. "No," I would reply as they tried to deliver a cup of stiff black tea to the interrogation room. "I will rough him up and get him to talk—just me and him alone. Give me three minutes."

I knew that any Iraqi man despises a slap in the face because it makes him feel like a girl. That was my first move, a humiliating slap. As the man slumped, still uncooperative, I would then taunt him with a threat, saying, "I know where your family lives."

Tactics like this were usually sufficient to prompt a confession, and I certainly had no intention of applying any of the torturous methods that the former regime had standardized. Exerting intimidating authority was not the same as inflicting inhumane harm on another man. Once they started to speak, the men would eventually divulge their ammunition sources and the location of their backup cohorts. I was proud to put my background to good use and had no tolerance for other Iraqi interpreters who put my country to shame by mocking, laughing, or deliberately making mistakes. This was the theater of war, not a playground.

Sincere as I was about my duties, I still had a humorous streak for moments when I was not conducting official business. Sometimes when I oriented a new Iraqi recruit in the chow hall at the base, I would create my own amusement. The food was foreign and unfamiliar to them, so I would escort the new soldiers through the line, helping them to identify the American menu. "These are beans, these are peas," I would say, pointing at the steaming tubs of food.

As we moved along in line past each tub, the men would pause and ask, "Pig?" They wanted assurance that they were not eating anything containing pork, the forbidden meat in Muslim culture.

"No," I would reply, "no pig."

Then, when we passed a platter piled with obscure crispy strips of fried meat, I would make no comment. Curious, hungry, and oblivious, the men would take a few pieces of bacon, the fatty aroma tantalizing. Tasting it, they would inevitably exclaim about the delicious American delicacy.

Only later would they find out that I had smugly let them eat pork, a blatant offense in the world of Islam. It was a harmless deception as far as I was concerned, as I was not terribly devoted to the dietary guidelines of the religious creed of my heritage. After doing this more than once, I gained a new nickname: Pig. I shrugged it off with a grin, preferring to focus on the mission at hand, which was certainly a serious one.

One of my assignments while serving with this particular platoon was pursuing a terrorist who had planted countless IEDs on the regional roads. We raided his house about thirty times. In each attempt, we would see him enter the house, and then he would mysteriously disappear once we barged through the front door. It was mystifying. The terrorist's sisters would scream when we kicked the door open, apparently alarmed and yet actually creating a distraction. Search after search, we could never spot a trace of him, not even a distant dot on the horizon fleeing out of our reach.

Once, we gained access to the roof of the terrorist's house, and his brother down below on the ground emerged, trying to deter us. The US lieutenant fired a round of bullets to scare the brother, which prompted him to holler the name of Allah. Swearing in the name of Allah is a very common way to try to get out of something, an escape mechanism that seeks to instill fear and command respect. It was a pathetic excuse to divert our attention.

We caused no harm to his family, nor did we ever find the tricky IED emplacer. Two of his bombs even hit the side of our Humvee, each incident a near miss that could easily have snuffed out my life. Much later, we found out from the terrorist's cousin that every time we entered the house, he would sneak out a back door and hide in the chicken coop while his sisters were shrieking to mask his scurrying footsteps. We had certainly seen that coop, a tiny structure seemingly far too small for any man to fit inside. If only we had prodded further, we would have found the rodent who knew how to burrow bombs in the ground and gnaw his way out of any chase.

I also became an improvised language tutor. One of the US sergeants was eager to learn some Arabic, although his willingness to learn a few key words was coupled with a dicey sense of humor. Prudence is a prerequisite in wartime, and his words were preceded by a lack of forethought.

At his insistence, I taught the sergeant how to say "Blow me up." It was not the smartest thing I had ever done. I never guessed that he would use his one sentence of Arabic for a foolishly devastating purpose. In the evening, that very same day, we were out on the road near Hussein's birthday palace in Tikrit, and the sergeant yelled loudly, in his best attempt at a local accent, "Blow me up!"

Instantaneously, an IED hit us. The red-hot device veered off course just enough at the last second so that we were not scorched. Looking in the direction of the source, we saw a man peering at us through a window in a house along the road. We rushed to the property, and as we blazed toward the building, the suspect locked the front door.

It was a metal door, as irritating and staunch as the rascal who stood on the other side of it. None of us wanted to contend with that unyielding metal. Holding a 12-gauge short shotgun, I screamed, "Come open the door or I will shoot!"

When I heard no sound of a bolt turning, I breached the door with the gun, my movements so abrupt and forceful that the cowering man had no moment to run. Grabbing the insurgent by the collar, I thrust him on the floor, cursing. "I will shoot you!" I shouted, bristling with indignation. My blood churned, a stew of annoyance with this daring IED emplacer who had almost succeeded in blowing me up, prompted by the sergeant's careless words.

"Did you plant this IED?" I asked him. The man's family watched as I glared at the man who was now reduced to a nervous mess at my feet. Their hysterical tears were like a cold sweat of fear, blended with a sorry attempt to beg for leniency.

We arrested the man, finding no other suspect after a conclusive search of the surrounding area. The sergeant learned his Arabic lesson that day. He also got a rasping reprimand for not taking seriously the severity of war. I was not accused of any wrongdoing for teaching someone a volatile sentence; rather, the experience taught me personally to keep my head in the game, which was no game at all. Being an Iraqi in a wartime arena on behalf of the US military was a privilege that I never took lightly. It was the pursuit of life.

CHAPTER ELEVEN

The US lieutenant who had brought me to the Remagen base and led our platoon spoke highly of me to his superiors, recommending that they use my skills even more fully. He recognized that my Iraqi background and my experience as a sniper were valuable assets to the multinational force. The authorities agreed, assigning me to the 101st Bravo Battery 3/320th Field Artillery as a personal interpreter for one of the US captains and as an active participant in air assault missions and raids.

While the raids were acts of aggression intended to quell the atrocities of terrorists, we also conducted knock and talk missions on foot, designed to gather information from the local population. These engagements were generally much more informal and friendly, in the best interest of the community. We would approach a door, knock, and wait for the resident to open the door. "Hello," we would say in a cordial greeting, "how is life for you today?"

A brief hello was the usual response, and we would add, "We are here to gather information." The people would be hesitant until they could see that we truly had peaceful intentions. Probing further, we would ask them, "Do you like our presence here? What can we do to make your life easier?"

Without fail, those questions would open the floodgates for a barrage of requests. Almost always, the locals would ask for water and electricity, as their impoverished living conditions lacked even the basic necessities. We had containers of clothing and shoes for the children, as well as school supplies. A pencil, an eraser, a paper notebook—these were treasures in the eyes of disadvantaged children. Sometimes, the terrorists even blew up school buildings to prevent the younger generations from the possibility of receiving an education. Our teams would build schools, determining that the cemented classrooms would establish stability in the present and hope for the future of a country beleaguered by war.

In my role as the captain's interpreter, I attended meetings at the governmental council level as well as tribal assemblies, seeking to promote a posture of peace in every intervention. The tribal nature of Iraqi society infuses the actions and relations of individuals in an organic, intangible way, as family authority influences every member to think twice before acting independently. Our primary purpose in the tribal dimension was to prudently prevent the leaders from instigating an eruption of violence. I also sought to glean knowledge about the sources of the IEDs that were a perpetual plague throughout the territory. The order of the day was to develop ties and nurture an atmosphere in which the future of Iraq could flourish. Sometimes it was as simple as equipping a tribal leader with resources that would enhance his reputation and visibility, encouraging him to defend the good of the society. While Operation Iraqi Freedom had begun with an abrupt air attack, the ensuing labor on the ground was a gradual, progressive effort that required persistence. The secret ingredient of any success could only be willing collaboration, and I was proud to be a thriving example that it was possible.

Not every day was so mild. The helicopter assaults were purposefully aimed at status-based targets, such as clusters of terrorists in the area of Samarra and Tikrit. On one of our expeditions, we targeted Hussein's cousin in Auja, arriving in three helicopters, generating a dusty wind that spattered the buildings below us like a spray of sharp needles. We penetrated his house through the roof and bound him with ropes, a tight circumscription to shorten the leash on unrestrained hegemony.

A nighttime air expedition took us south of Balad, an agricultural area where the terrorists were as sinuous as the serpentine grapevines and more acidic than the sweet citrus groves that dotted the landscape. We arrived in several helicopters, resolved to locate and capture terrorists, focusing first on finding a surface to land our aircraft. The cultivated fields were not smooth, and even the desert was not as flat as it appeared.

I was in a helicopter with five other people, with one man between the door and me. As we began to touch down on the ground, one of the helicopter's rear wheels hit a narrow ditch, causing all of us to tilt precariously like a camel awkwardly kneeling for its rider to dismount. We held onto the seats and anything else within reach as the helicopter rocked back and forth uncontrollably on the verge of an unbridled crash. My heart was in my underwear in utter desperation, and I thought that for sure we would not crawl out of the wreckage alive. Maneuvering quickly, the pilot lifted the helicopter into the air and managed to resume a steady flight, landing at another location. I was well aware that my life had once again been spared even as the war advanced, dragging casualties in tow.

On another assignment to seize terrorists, I traveled in a Humvee with a US captain from the 101st Bravo Battery 3/320th and a few others, while our partner team flew in an Apache helicopter. It was still daylight, late afternoon, and when we arrived at the designated location, the suspects were nowhere to be found. Our captain instructed us to initiate conversations with the neighbors in an effort to cull further clues about the trail of the terrorists. As we were beginning to do so, the pilot in the helicopter, still hovering overhead, contacted us sternly via radio, announcing that three terrorists were approaching in a white pickup truck with red stripes along the side. They were only a quarter mile away, pressing toward our platoon on the ground.

"What do we do?" the pilot asked the captain, who was standing next to me.

Exuding confidence, the captain ordered, "Fire a warning shot." Any average driver would stop at the sound of a bullet.

The pilot fired a shot, activating the Apache helicopter's 30mm machine gun with a visual cue from the lenses of his helmet. Intrepid in spite of the gunfire, the pickup truck plowed forward toward us. With increased urgency, the captain commanded, "Go ahead and engage."

As the pilot fired more shots, the driver of the pickup truck turned his wheel to the side, rolling off the road into a ditch to avoid being pelted. Those of us on the ground were about twenty yards away from the truck, and we shot bullets at the frame of the truck to instill upon the detoured men the seriousness of the skirmish. Pausing for a half breath after pulling the trigger, we ran in that direction to drag the driver out of the truck, as well as the two other men who accompanied him, all three of them the terrorists whom we had been hunting. In the clatter, a bullet fired from the helicopter penetrated the chest of one of the terrorists, and through the awful, bloody hole I could see his heart beating its final pulse. I got no satisfaction from this sight and wished that we could have avoided such an extreme end. The other two men survived, and we took them into custody.

Before leaving the scene, we searched the truck for any evidence of illegal activity. The hidden stash left no room for doubt, as we unearthed suicide vests, grenades, AK-47s, and satellite phones, the common form of undercover communication for insurgent Iraqis. We had been mere paces away from becoming the victims of the very men whom we intended to capture.

Ushering the two men back to the base, we listened to their cries for help and their begging to see their families. There was no mercy for this kind of request since they refused to cooperate and unveil any information about their schemes. Although we had no desire to pamper these rebellious men, we did want to treat them humanely, so Army doctors evaluated their injuries and bandaged their wounds. It had been a rough day for all of us, another episode in a campaign that was anything but commonplace.

Not every mission was a shining success. One day, we were flying in a Black Hawk helicopter over the farmlands of Tikrit, well aware of the risk that our bird in the sky could refract a glint of sunshine and publicize our presence to any enemy on the ground. As we flew over a village, the danger became palpable when someone with an AK-47 started to shoot at the helicopter. The pilot initiated an impromptu descent above a swampy field, remaining six feet in the air so that we could jump out of the aircraft.

The first soldier hurtled courageously through the gaping helicopter door and got stuck in the mud, huddled in a grimy mess. The others wanted to use his back as a landing pad, but I squelched that idea so that they would not unwittingly break our own buddy's spine. So, each of us jumped, our feet sinking into the muck until we were up to our knees in mud, and then we painstakingly tromped toward dry land. Eventually, we reached firm footing and secured the area, searching for the individual who was shooting at the helicopter. The pilot fired flares toward the shooter, catching a glimpse of his gun, which was a shorter AK-47 rifle. This led us to believe that he was an insurgent leader, as men like Osama bin Laden often carried compact rifles as a sign of their authority. As the pilot gave us directions via radio, we pursued the suspect but lost sight of him in the farmland. Some of the flares veered off toward the nearby houses, getting far too close to some children, even burning their skin. Our quest was not worth that type of injury, and we admitted that it was time to abandon the day's attempt.

Not every chapter in war ends in victory, and yet I was not about to quit. There was always the prospect of triumph around the next corner. I was on a quest to extinguish the insurgency, while also fanning the flames of my own search for meaning as a man.

CHAPTER TWELVE

In the beginning of 2007, the US military reassigned me to the 2-505 Eighty-Second Airborne, transferring me to Camp Speicher, a larger base for multiple units in the Tikrit region. I worked for Bravo Company as an interpreter alongside two great men, a lieutenant and a sergeant, assisting them to assess locations for potential sniper missions. Their previous interpreter was fired for misconduct, so I arrived with the purpose of grabbing the baton and running the relay race with the best agility that I could marshal. With my police and SWAT experience, it was a seamless transition, as I could naturally identify nefarious individuals, a task that was more challenging for the foreign military forces. The subtlest Iraqi mannerisms were significant to my native eyes, and my new American comrades trusted my keen gaze.

In between scouting expeditions, our banter was sometimes lighthearted, sometimes grave, sometimes somewhere in the middle where the meaning of life hovers. Sgt. Gray in particular was intriguingly distinct from the common soldier, and it was not merely because he was the platoon leader. He was intelligent and friendly, yet more soft-spoken than the others. Gentleness like his was not a normal trait in the company of trained fighters. I was curious to know why.

What distinguished Sgt. Gray the most was an uncanny habit. He always carried a small book in a pocket above his knee, pulling it out whenever he had a brief break. Other soldiers carried similar books and trinkets as good luck charms, but he treated his as if it were more than a superstition. It was a tattered paperback with a camouflage cover wrapped in duct tape to keep it intact. The edges were dingy, not from the dust of the Iraqi desert but from the fingers of a devoted reader. It was obviously something special, though I had absolutely no idea what book could keep his attention that much. I determined to ask him about it someday, although I was in no hurry.

During that same period, I picked up a book from a shelf of free items where soldiers left soaps, candies, and other treats that they had received in care packages and did not want to keep for themselves. The surplus shelf was enticing because I never received packages until later that year when one of the US soldiers completed his tour and started mailing me beef jerky. I occasionally browsed to see if anything on the shelf appealed. The book that I picked was in English, and I was always eager to expand my language abilities to be a better interpreter. I did not notice or even care about the title or the author, only the language. Improving my English was a valuable life skill even though my superiors insisted that my fluency was excellent. I wanted to know more. I watched discarded DVDs of *The Andy Griffith Show* or anything else that would teach me the tricks of speaking like any American citizen.

I had never read a whole book in English before, and this one stumped me. It was not the language that baffled me—it was the peculiar format. Each of the pages was arranged in columns, different from any of the textbooks I had used in school. The page headings were names of people, men such as Peter, Timothy, Luke, Mark, Matthew. Flipping through the book casually, I noticed a long section where every page had the name John at the top. Since I knew several soldiers named John, I decided I would start there. An irresistible compulsion guided me to those particular pages, an urge that I would only understand later. I began reading from right to left and backward, as I would in Arabic, my eyes trailing from the first paragraph at the top of the second column and then over to the first paragraph at the top of the first column. Then I would shift to the second column again, bouncing back and forth. It made no sense; the thoughts lacked flow. I quit.

Then one day, when Sgt. Gray was engrossed in his trusty book again, leaning against a Humvee, I walked past him close enough to quickly glance at the open page. I was sly, unnoticed. As my eyes brushed the page, I saw what looked like a chapter heading: John.

The apparent coincidence shocked me. Turning to face him fully, I said, "Hey!" my eagerness uncontained, "What are you reading?"

"A Bible," he responded with a smile, seemingly excited that I had asked.

"How do you read that book?" I asked with a hint of perplexity and frustration.

Looking confused, Sgt. Gray replied, "What do you mean?"

"I cannot understand anything in it," I said, convinced that the book was at fault.

Thoughtfully, Sgt. Gray asked me how I had been reading the book. Pointing with my finger, I showed him how I had followed the text from right to left, skipping across the columns.

"It makes no sense," I insisted, bewildered and wondering why he bothered reading the Bible so desperately, as if his life depended on it.

Sgt. Gray laughed, thoroughly tickled under the guise of his bulky military garb. "No, man," he said between chuckles, "you need to read it this way."

Staying on that same page in the section labeled John, Sgt. Gray demonstrated how to read the English verses, descending the entire first column on the left and then the second column. The sentences started to seem more significant, the words flowing one after another as if written by an eloquent speechwriter. Each verse captivated me, and I did not want the impromptu instruction to end

Since I had my own copy and now knew how to crisscross

through the columns without getting dizzy, I started to read the Bible every day. I stayed in the chapters of John, going to Sgt. Gray whenever I had questions about unusual concepts and characters. One night, I came across this puzzling statement: "I am the good shepherd. The good shepherd lays down his life for the sheep" (John 10:11).

This seemed utterly strange. I knew from the experience of shepherding my father's cousin's flock in the desert of Ad-Dawr that sheep are dirty, stinky, stupid, the lowest of animals. I knew that they were valuable livestock, but I never wanted to get close to them, let alone die for them. Sheep disgusted me. The thought nagged at my conscience because I knew that Jesus was the one talking, claiming that he was a good shepherd who knows his sheep one by one. Anything Jesus said deserved some respectful scrutiny. His was the name that had suddenly come to my mind on the day when I had survived the wretched car bomb in front of the police academy in Tikrit. I could not ignore Jesus.

But, sheep? There was no shame in asking, and the devout sergeant was always open to field my questions. I prodded him with honest questions about the absurdity of the sheep metaphor. He explained that Jesus is the Lamb of God and that we are his followers, the sheep. The Lamb came into the world to die and save people from sin, because he was the only one qualified to sacrifice his life. I absorbed every word intently.

"If Jesus is the Lamb who died, how can he be the Shepherd too?" I asked. Sgt. Gray explained more about Jesus as the Son of God, and I began to slowly understand that this famous prophet was more than a teacher. He had done something for me personally in the past, and I longed to explore his whole identity. I could sense that Jesus was bigger than I had ever imagined.

Admittedly, I equated Jesus with Christianity, its connotations copious. And I equated Christianity with the United States, the country of Texas, the land of my aspirations. I naively thought that anyone who lived there would have the designation "Christian" on their birth certificate, just like my Iraqi certificate indicated that I was Muslim. Maybe I could get a document that called me a Christian, too, gaining access to the opportunity to live up to my nickname, Tex. Although I was sincerely curious about Jesus, I had some mixed motives and confusion, and I was still an arrogant and adept sniper. I knew I was good, or so I thought. But I was also rude, disrespectful, and full of hatred. I got along well with my military companions but had no tolerance for the insurgents, despising them as worse than the smelly sheep that Jesus described.

Sgt. Gray had wisdom beyond his years and coached me through my inquisitive trek. I valued his insights and developed a steady friendship with him, this fascinating platoon leader who had a soft heart. His knowledge of Jesus was eye-opening to me, and I related to the blind man whose story John told in the chapter before the gripping account of the sheep. Jesus touched the blind man in a miraculous way, transforming his life with the gift of sight, then opening the eyes of his spirit so that he could encounter Jesus with a greater depth of understanding. It was a story of blindness followed by belief. It all seemed so foreign to me, not only because I was reading in English but because I had never heard about worshiping Jesus.

When Jesus found the blind man again after their encounter, their exchange was alluring.

> Jesus asked, "Do you believe in the Son of Man?"
>
> "Who is he, sir?" the man asked. "Tell me so that I may believe in him."
>
> Jesus said, "You have now seen him; in fact, he is the one speaking with you."
>
> Then the man said, "Lord, I believe," and he worshiped him. (John 9:35-38)

It was as if the words in the Bible were customized to my quest for meaning. I read about the Jews cross-examining Jesus, unsure of his real identity. Interrogation was one of my specialties, and I was puzzled when I encountered Jesus in these verses of John. Who was he, really? Why were some people worshiping him? "The Jews who were there gathered around him, saying, 'How long will you keep us in suspense? If you are the Messiah, tell us plainly'" (John 10:24). Lamb, Shepherd, Son of Man, Messiah—Jesus made bold and confusing claims. The Jews accused him of blasphemy, an ominous offense. The allegations could have repulsed me as mere madness, but they were too compelling to reject prematurely.

The more I read, the more I wanted to know. I kept prying Sgt. Gray for clarity to satisfy my curiosity, and he told me that he was praying for me. He also confided that a church of Christians in Texas was praying that God would protect me in the war and help me to grasp the things I was reading in the Bible. Instead of feeling uncomfortable with the idea of Christian prayers directed specifically at me, I welcomed it. It felt like a love that I had never experienced.

CHAPTER THIRTEEN

As the weeks passed from winter to spring of 2007, our Eighty-Second Airborne platoon moved temporarily to Patrol Base Woodcock in the Ad-Dawr area where my father had lived in his youth. The base was named after a sergeant who had died as the result of an explosion while he was serving in March, yet another casualty in the tense terrain where we operated. In late May, my father visited me at the base, a risky choice because any overt association with the US military, even a short-lived stopover to see his son, could cause the Iraqi community to suspect him of collaborating with the infidel. I was already rejected by my Iraqi compatriots back home in Samarra, and my father was treading on dangerous territory. In addition, my responsibilities required me to perform duties that increased the angst of the surrounding community. Not long before my father's visit, I had detained one of his former drinking buddies, a man who had a connection with terrorist schemes. While confronting the enemy of terrorism, I had stirred up more antagonism, and my father's support for my mission also implicated him.

Despite the asphyxiating apprehension that dominated the desert air, my father arrived with his trademark broad smile, preferring cordiality over conflict. His earnest desire to see me was stronger than his caution in the wartime environment, and he showed up unannounced. I was in a meeting when he came, and I ran to the gate when my superiors notified me that I had a special visitor. The grin that always washed over his face was a characteristic that I had gladly inherited, and my smile matched his.

As I approached, I could see a party of three waiting for me: my father, my mother, and my little brother Aaftab, who was barely a toddler. Excitement mixed with embarrassment deep in my gut. No tough soldier hosts his mother on the front lines of a grueling war. Tumbling around with those emotions was the stern conviction that my mother's worry would only increase upon observing the vulnerability of our conditions. I had never told her about the car bomb that I had survived in Tikrit, not wanting to add a heart attack in my own home to the death toll of the unnerving days that all of us were enduring. So, I allowed my smile to warm the edges of the rough encounter. Above all, I was thrilled to see them, noticing with amusement that Aaftab seemed shy, startled by the brusque uniform that squared my shoulders in contrast with my father's fluid turban.

I proudly introduced my father to Sgt. Gray and the lieutenant who were my leaders, my friends, my guides in the desert wilderness where I had once led my father's sheep. My father was pleased to be assured that I was honoring his wishes, serving as a man in support of the US military. The encounter was brief. Prolonging the visit would have meant endangering the safety of my family, and none of us wanted to increase the already looming jeopardy. The lieutenant pulled out a perk to sweeten our smiles—a Dum Dums lollipop for Aaftab.

"Eat it now," the lieutenant told my brother nonchalantly, pretending that it was a prize to be savored immediately simply for its own sake. "Toss the wrapper away before you leave the base." I interpreted every word, grasping what was behind his instructions. The lieutenant wanted to sound casual, but his motive was exact.

Even the most mundane activity was subject to protocols. The lieutenant knew that a stray American candy wrapper, if seen in the hands of an Iraqi toddler, could all too easily mark a trail back to its source. It was imperative that Aaftab not take any souvenir back into the streets of Samarra. My mother topped off the farewell exchange by giving me a container that she had brought from her kitchen. Tucked inside, wrapped in a cloth to keep them moist, was a sugary stash of homemade *kleicha* cookies, the aroma of dough filled with cardamom-infused date pulp wafting to my dusty nostrils when I popped open a corner of the lid. I hugged her, kissed her, tried to stand tall and not succumb to memories of home.

"See you later," I said to Aaftab, kissing his lollipop-smeared cheek as my mother held him close, his stubby legs wrapped around her hips. I did not know when later would be, nor did I want to consider the possibility that later might never happen. A hopeful outlook was the only way to withstand the uncertainty. My father rejoined us after stepping aside to talk momentarily with the commander, and it was time for my family to retrace their steps outside the gate and catch a taxi.

"Thank you for coming," I told my father. "Please be safe." There was nothing more to say, only watch them walk purposefully down the road. I knew that staring wistfully as they disappeared on the desert horizon was an option, but the duty of the day also called me. It was May of 2007, and the horizon was dark all over Iraq.

Within days, Sgt. Gray, who was my platoon leader, and a select few from the squad went on a sniper mission, driving in a Humvee with no headlights or flicker of any kind so that the enemy could not spot us. About half a mile from the location where we planned to mount our operation for the night, we exited the vehicle. Sgt. Gray ordered me to call the Iraqi Army soldiers who were nearby and command them not to shoot as we approached. In that instant, they fired.

Grabbing the radio, I yelled again, "Stop! We are the United States Army," I announced. "We are coming to your location."

The Iraqi Army commander had already received advance notice of our arrival but seemed ill-equipped to contain the agitation of soldiers who were skeptical of any US military intervention. After a pause, an Iraqi soldier replied via radio, "OK, come."

I accompanied Sgt. Gray as we scaled a hill where the Iraqi soldiers were planted. When we reached the summit, one of the Iraqis thrust a machine gun toward Sgt. Gray, jabbing the barrel into his face. Sgt. Gray stood still, keenly assessing the menace.

Before anyone could utter a threat, I slapped the gun away from Sgt. Gray's cheek, irritation erupting in my clenched fist. I wanted to empty this festering pocket of Iraqi disdain for the US presence; I wanted to force these soldiers to respect the US military and allow us to introduce solutions to appease the animosity that reigned throughout the country. My fury peaking, I beat up the Iraqi soldier, blow after blow.

Sgt. Gray stopped me with a strong verbal order. I was frustrated, yearning to retaliate against this Iraqi soldier who had treated us with such overt contempt and disrespect. He had tried to kill us, and I thought he deserved a dose of his own insolence. My pulse escalated, but I obeyed the command and lowered my arms.

We turned our focus toward the purpose of the mission, preparing for the sniper attack. Less than three minutes had passed when the same irreverent Iraqi soldier asked Sgt. Gray if he had any water. The request was so audacious, even my own thirsty tongue quivered.

To my astonishment, Sgt. Gray gave him the only bottle of water that he had brought for the night. This sergeant, a clear-minded platoon leader whose undeniable strength in battle always coexisted with the book he kept in his pocket, must be crazy. "Dude," I blurted out, "he almost killed us, and now you are giving him water?"

"That is what Jesus did for us," Sgt. Gray said pensively. "He sacrificed."

I shook my head, contemplating but not comprehending. Prohibiting me from beating up the Iraqi soldier was not the first time that Sgt. Gray had to reprimand me for my arrogance toward the local people. He always did it privately and with kindness, as if his courteous temperament were a pleasant scent carried on a breeze from a foreign land. I was rude and resented being regarded by the Iraqis as a traitor. The hatred that brewed in my heart was a poisonous cauldron compared with the mild nature of my platoon leader. How could a strong sergeant be so generous, both to me and to them? Whatever the reason, I sensed that his unique character had less to do with a difference in nationality and more to do with who he was as a person. I just could not figure it out.

Each day was decisive, with little time for the leisure to discuss life's existential questions. The long-beards were gathering from all over the Middle East, ready to die, and we were constantly on edge, pivoting to apply the rules of engagement to each iteration of the accentuated hostility throughout Iraq. Sixteen days after the nighttime sniper mission, back at the base, my captain summoned me urgently.

"Tex, you need to call home," he said, passing my cell phone to me.

"Thanks," I replied. "I will call later."

There was no rush to check in with Samarra while absorbed in my activities at the base. I had left my cell phone with the captain while on an assignment, having no need for it while on duty. The captain did not let me be so dismissive and explained that the phone had rung incessantly. Wondering about the unusual stream of missed calls, he had decided to answer.

"Abbas, Abbas," a young woman's voice pleaded. The captain did not recognize the name, so he consulted a list of soldiers stationed at the base and determined that her insistence was directed toward me, Tex.

Pointing again at the cell phone in my hands, the captain urged, "You need to call them now."

CHAPTER FOURTEEN

The captain returned to his command post, leaving me with my cell phone and a lingering curiosity about what sort of excitement or emergency was happening back home in Samarra. I dialed promptly, and just as rapidly, my sister Amara answered. She told me that our father had gone to heaven.

"You are joking," I said, a wavering smile breaking loose on my face, just like my father's grin when he had waved goodbye at the base only a few days previously.

"No," she said, her voice trembling like my now vacillating lips. "He actually died."

"I need to go," I asserted, stupefied, a staggering shock preventing me from letting her speak further. I hung up. The summer heat was suddenly as lukewarm as my heart, the desert dryness a vacuum sucking away my breath. I retreated to the barracks, my bravado withering, and wept.

With every cry, with every dispirited teardrop, my chest echoed, feeling the emptiness of a world where my father was not. We had never been close, nor had I ever truly experienced his affection, except that things had started to change. When he had visited the base, I had seen how proud he was of my position in the US military, and it had reminded me of our shopping excursion after his release from prison. I longed for his embrace, just like the tightly knit fibers of the sweater he had bought for me that day. He had been transformed in prison, and the sweater was a gesture of the warm care that he struggled to express. Now, it was all unraveling.

I had not given my sister a chance to tell me how my father had died. For all I knew, he could have been struck by a sudden illness or slipped away in his sleep. She had only said that he had gone to heaven, the logical destiny of a man who had chosen the path of goodness and trust in God after the agony of solitary confinement. Only later did I learn the facts of the tragedy.

My family soon told me that men had swept into our family home in Samarra and shot my father, killing him. Their motive was to eliminate a traitor. I learned that my father had been spying on behalf of my battalion because we had lost a lot of men in the war. He joined the police force and used his rank to gather terrorist information, which he then disclosed to the US military, revealing details about weaponry arsenals and insurgent locations. It was an act of love on his part, a salute of patriotism in support of the US mission and a grand but confidential display of concern for my success. I never got to thank him, and I never got to say goodbye. It was impossible to attend his funeral, due to security ramifications, making his abrupt death seem excruciatingly impalpable. My father was now forever out of reach.

My crushing cries were already dissolving into anger, stunned as I was that my father's life had been plucked away. Within a few hours, my captain entered the barracks, interrupting my bitter tears. My roommate had told the other men about my grief, and the authorities evaluated my situation quickly, declaring that I could not leave the base by myself because of my emotional state. I had the option of going with the company on a mission for a couple of months or staying at the base. The captain was wary that I might make a grave mistake if left alone, acting out of vengeance for my father's murder.

"Stay on the base or come with me," my captain said, offering no other alternative.

"I really have no choice," I replied, agreeing with him. "I will go with you."

It was early June 2007, and I went with my captain to a base where the US military was preparing to launch a direct intervention to deter the infernal insurgency. Al-Qaeda had instituted a lockdown in the city of Baqubah, in the Diyala province, and the tension was unfathomable. Their tactics were audacious, the air so charged with explosivity that every sense in our bodies was on alert. They invented an inconceivable tactic that depended on the eruptive capacity of ammonium nitrate. The procedure began with gutting old refrigerators, filling them with the chemical compound, rigging the machine with wiring, and then burying the bomb under the roadways. Because of their corrupt connections with the local leaders, they even devised a paving program, covering the explosive refrigerators with asphalt in hopes that a large troop carrier would drive over the spot. Detonating hidden bombs was their ideal method for eliminating US adversaries literally from the ground upward. But we would not withdraw.

The US military concluded that it was time for us to act on the offensive. Operation Arrowhead Ripper began June 19, aiming to subdue insurgents and secure the city of Baqubah. In the night, we broadcast a clear message, proclaiming, "Do not lock your doors or we will break in." Early the next morning, we set out in armored strikers, six men per vehicle, going house to house on a hunt for the enemy.

Despite the announcement, the first door we confronted was locked. The man inside was so frightened that he could not figure out how to unlock the door, and that was not an acceptable excuse in the face of our operation. We detonated the door, with shrapnel flying. Each successive house was a similar barrier, and each hour was excruciatingly hot. I was always appointed as the third man to enter when breaching a house, a strategic decision to shield me from the up-front danger. My SWAT skills were vital to our advancement, and the US military wanted to calculate victories, not victims. In the ensuing days, we raided 2,500 houses, with fifteen men in each platoon. I was fuming with anger from my father's death and had no consideration for the Iraqis, even the local citizens. As my blood boiled underneath my desert-toned camouflage uniform, I smoked and chewed tobacco, survival mechanisms to numb the angst and fuel my raging frame. Our water supply was too hot to drink, and we tallied fifteen casualties due to the excessive heat. Improvising to avoid dehydration, we administered fluids to each other intravenously, two bags per day. The tobacco certainly did not soothe the soaring temperature in my body, but I could not care less. My father was gone, the terrorists were howling presumptuously, and my only urge was to punish the enemy, stomping on them like the cigarette butts that kept me from giving in to my grief more completely.

Some of the houses were booby traps, the doors a false facade of hospitality hiding a web of wires. The instant we touched the surface of the door, it would blow up in a fiery resistance to our attempts to tame the embers of the enemy. We learned to look for any cables or ramshackle construction, and we employed overhead thermal vision techniques to detect sources of heat inside the houses. Any hot spot could be a fermenting explosive rather than a welcoming hearth fire.

One day at around 11:30 a.m., after a draining morning of raids, we stopped in the middle of a block at a house where we intended to pause for a few hours. It was a standard procedure for the US military to request permission to occupy a home, paying the residents to provide a shelter where we could be briefly refreshed. After searching the yard, we entered the house, receiving a positive response from the middle-aged couple in the entryway. However, they told us that one room was off-limits. That was unacceptable to me.

I ordered the man and woman to step aside to the corner of the main hall. My responsibility was to ensure that the home was safe before the soldiers could relax, so I insisted. The more I asked, the more they begged me not to open the door of the room, one of many that bordered the living space. I took possession of the man's rifle, bracing myself for further resistance in this home where instead of a cool cup of water I was given a cold shoulder. I searched the other rooms, noticing with disgust that there was a stool in the bathroom covered with bodily fluid.

As I progressed toward the locked room, the man jumped in front of the door, pleading, "Please, no."

Swearing with annoyance at his lack of hospitality, I told the soldiers to move the man and his wife out of my way, and then I barged into the room. In it was a narrow bed, its metal frame supporting a frail young woman, slumped on a worn sheet, her dark eyes gaping chasms of fear.

"What are you doing here?" I yelled.

"Please, sir," she said, her voice as fragile as her physique. "I cannot move."

I edged closer as she nodded with her head, pointing to her paralyzed arms and legs. Her listless limbs broke my heart. I turned back toward the doorway, where her parents peered into the room, trembling next to the soldiers who stood guard.

"What is going on with her?" I asked, trying to make sense of the miserable scene.

They told me that two years previously, their eighteen year-old daughter had returned home from school one day in full health, a hardy student, a beautiful young lady. The following morning, when she awoke, she could not move. The whole family was stupefied. Her devastation reminded me of how my aunt had two daughters with mental and physical disabilities, a heartrending daily ordeal.

"Why do you not take care of her, take her to a doctor?" I prodded the man of the house, frustrated with his failure as a father. Ashamed, he told me that he had tried, but a local doctor had diagnosed a damaged spinal cord which required surgery.

He had no money for any treatments. Irked with myself for falsely accusing him of negligence, I apologized for my attitude, passing the man's rifle back to his hesitant hands.

Our platoon needed to intervene, this time in an initiative of compassion. The family was so poor that they had subsisted on rice for the past six months and had not gotten fresh water for fifteen days. Their only source of water was the runoff from thunderstorms that they collected in the gutters and in large dishes in the yard. Despite the 125-degree heat, they sweltered with no electricity, no ventilation. I went with one of the lieutenants to buy five gallons of gas for their generator, activating a fan to ease the suffering of the wilting desert willow who sat hopelessly in bed. We provided rice and other basic provisions to fortify them— flour to make bread, dried chickpeas, canned tomato paste, and tea—for their languishing spirit of hospitality.

Seeing their plight, my mind wandered back to Samarra, and I started making comparisons, knowing that my mother and siblings knew nothing of the deprivation in Baqubah. In the midst of my painful grief, I could not ignore the fact that I was privileged. It seemed as if God was tapping me on the shoulder, inquisitively prodding, "I took your father, but your family has food and water, a safe home. Look at this family. What is your excuse?"

This time I was the one being interrogated. It caught me by surprise, and I was speechless, gripped with remorse for my cruelty. I had no excuse for being so mean. There was nothing to say in response to God's question, and nothing to do but acknowledge my faults. Instead of becoming a good man, I was veering off onto a malicious detour, and the afternoon of aiding the impoverished family exposed the poverty of my spirit. My contemplation would have continued, except that the commander ordered our platoon to move on to assist another team. There were still people to serve and battles to fight, and now I would be approaching it with a more attuned awareness. My motives needed to be right.

CHAPTER FIFTEEN

Our next objective after the series of house raids was to prepare for a firefight, a daunting prospect. Knowing that we were on the brink of a gunfire battle with the enemy required a deliberate strategy as well as a sharpened mental acuity. While I focused on my responsibility as an active member on the offensive, there were brief lulls between tactical sessions, allowing my mind to wander.

One afternoon, as we awaited our next engagement, the Iraqi army arrived at our location with a lunch of *bamia*, a richly seasoned tomato-based soup laden with lamb and okra. Savory and fortifying, it was a soothing watering hole for a company of hungry soldiers, even if it was not as good as my mother's rendition of the recipe. But I was less concerned with our provisions than with another sensation churning inside of me, making me pensive. While the men were still emptying their bowls, I walked away from the group and found Sgt. Gray.

"I hate my life; I hate who I have become," I told him. "How can I become a Christian?"

Sgt. Gray smiled and said, "Tell all of that to Jesus, and he will change your life."

The words on the pages of the Bible had long ago ceased to be an exercise in improving my mastery of English. They were words of life, and they applied to Americans, to Iraqis, to me. Sgt. Gray had taught me how to read each verse for myself, and now he prompted me to forgive my enemies and reach out directly to the author of the Bible. My anger was not just a character flaw, I realized—it was a symptom of the fact that I was a sinner. I needed help if I wanted to be a better person. It was time to call on the name of Jesus.

My intentions were interrupted when we received orders to cross the street and search a local auto mechanic shop for any evidence of foul play. It was far from pristine, more like a junkyard riddled with wrecked cars and spare parts, making me begin to wonder what might be lurking in a rusted trunk, underneath a hood, tucked in a dingy corner. As our platoon began to assess the tools and equipment throughout the large space, I noticed that the tanks, armored vehicles, and other friendly striker brigades that had accompanied us were starting to clear the area outside on the road. The abruptness of their evacuation alarmed me, so I approached the new lieutenant who was commanding our unit. He had arrived at the field with a bulk of head knowledge from his training, along with the arrogance to match it, while lacking practical experience. Presenting my alert as diplomatically as possible, I urged him to contact our captain and find out what was happening.

The lieutenant ignored my plea, resistant to any advice. Minutes elapsed as I prompted the others around me to realize that something unusual was unfolding. The friendly fleet of vehicles had left us in the dust of the mechanic shop. The radioman tried to contact our captain, but with each attempt, there was no response, only empty static. Finally, in a flurry of realization, one of the men said that the radio sequence had changed, stunting the communication. Pulling some notes from a previous notification, the radioman deciphered the correct code to call our captain. With this, the reply was immediate.

"Get out of there!" the captain said insistently over the radio. "You will get blown up." Twenty minutes beforehand, the command center had ordered an air strike on the mechanic shop, and the attack could hit at any instant. We ran for our lives.

116

Our earth shaking sprint spared us any casualties, and when we reached safer ground, the lieutenant was fired on the spot for putting our entire platoon in danger. We caught our breath only briefly as we moved on to the next location, planting ourselves in an agricultural area outside the city, poised for attack. We gained access to the roof of a house in the farmland and stayed there for a couple of hours while awaiting further instructions. Because the spare moment was precious, I stepped aside from the group and found a spot on the far edge of the roof where I could be alone.

Oblivious to my surroundings, I turned my attention to Jesus and prayed silently, asking him to enter my life, to forgive all of my sin. Only he could change me, only Jesus could make me a good man. "God, I want to be your son!" I cried, eager to be accepted by my eternal Father in heaven, longing to fill the void in my heart forever. I remembered what John had recorded in the Bible, where Jesus stated, "I am the way and the truth and the life. No one comes to the Father except through me" (John 14:6).

I had barely expressed my commitment when a forceful rumble invaded the airways. It inundated the entire atmosphere, a dynamic ear-shattering wave of turbulence, and I was certain that Jesus was taking me to heaven. Mortified and ecstatic, I jumped to my feet, my faith soaring above the skies. I had found what Jesus promised—the Way, the Truth, the Life. Heaven was happening now!

My holy elation turned to pure laughter when I looked up. The US military was performing a show of force with a fleet of F-16 fighter jets, flying low and loud to declare their presence. We had been notified beforehand that this would be happening at some point, but I had forgotten about it in the midst of my prayer to Jesus and my duties on the ground. I gathered my equipment and rejoined the group, ready for action, renewed in spirit.

The next morning, I went into the farming village with my squad for the purpose of demonstrating to the population that we had arrived on the scene. Belligerence would be their choice, not ours. I had already told Sgt. Gray about the previous night's experience, and he was as thrilled as I was about my expression of faith, laughing with me about my startled reaction to the F-16 jets that were not there to transport me to heaven. I felt so relieved to be free from the burden of hatred that had been weighing on me more than my military gear. One of the other sergeants saw that my countenance was different, my brooding scowl erased.

"Tex, wipe that smile off your face," he said. "What is wrong with you?" It was obvious that I had changed, and no one could deny the fact that a soldier who smiles in the face of war is an anomaly. It was supernatural.

There was no leisure to talk as we began to conduct a foot patrol of the village. Two or three bullets shot in our direction, near misses. We started chasing the culprits, running toward a cluster of small houses in a sweltering pursuit. Seeing one of the doors swung wide open, I rushed inside, stopping abruptly when I saw an elderly man sitting in the main living space. His two sons stood nearby, able-bodied young men who stared at me with the dread of innocence, apprehensive that I might accuse them of firing the shots. Near them, propped to the side, were two AK-47s, as dusty as the few pieces of furniture that hugged the walls.

The sergeant who had been mystified by my smile that morning followed me into the house. Unfortunately, he witnessed an eruption of my annoyance, my grin vanishing as my lips spewed out a stream of curses. Having narrowly escaped one of the bullets, I was agitated and began to yell at the man and his sons, questioning them in Arabic and swearing profusely in English. As they responded calmly to my interrogation, I soon realized that they had nothing to do with the skirmish in the streets, and my temper cooled.

As I shifted my stance, ready to retreat through the open door, the meek man looked at me intently, raising his index finger to pose a question. With sincere curiosity, he asked, "What does motherf***er mean?"

My chin dipped down toward my chest, and I turned toward the sergeant. "You tell him," I said. The soldier in authority over me refused to speak.

I looked back at the Iraqi man who waited earnestly for the answer to his question. "It is a bad word," I said. "Don't worry about it."

"I am an English teacher," the man replied. "I want to learn."

My spirit cringed. God convicted me in that instant, revealing to me that as his son, I could not be using foul language like this. Embarrassed, I apologized to the older man for my bad-mouthed recklessness. It was a defining moment in my life because I realized that God was starting to change me, shaping my attitudes and channeling my desires. Anything less than honoring God was despicable, and my heart wanted only to walk in the way of goodness.

CHAPTER SIXTEEN

The summer of 2007 blazed onward, with Operation Arrowhead Ripper confronting the volatility of terrorism in Baqubah sometimes with positive effect, sometimes suffering explosive individual losses. The defeat of al-Qaeda in the city was imminent. As June surged into July and then into August, every day was an exhausting fight for survival.

On my last mission, I was assigned to join a company in clearing out another village that the terrorists still stubbornly controlled. A new soldier arrived to bolster our numbers, a young man who had been expelled from another company due to misbehavior. Our task was to keep a close eye on him.

We approached the area in helicopters, with friendlies discharging mortar rounds ahead of us to establish our arrival. Beyond that, we had artillery hitting the bigger targets. The terrorists, desperate and fierce, shot at us feverishly, unwilling to relent. We succeeded in landing safely, clearing the surrounding area and advancing to the village.

The gunfire did not diminish as we entered the village. As we passed a barn, the new soldier on our team alarmed all of us, claiming that there were people inside. He tossed a fragmentation grenade at the barn, exhibiting a bravado that soon proved pointless. What he had thought was a cluster of evildoers was one very petrified cow whose skeleton disintegrated as chestnut-brown fur flew like sparks.

We moved on, entering one of the houses and beginning to question a man whose odd gaze exuded culpability. His two-year-old daughter toddled around the floor near his feet, her playfulness spoiled by the sight of soldiers in uniform invading her unstable haven. Reticent to communicate, the man seemed to be hiding something. However, the more I initiated conversation, the more I recognized that he had an intellectual disability. With reduced harshness, I ordered the man to sit down and keep his daughter next to him. The new soldier watched as I addressed the man with caution, assessing the atmosphere for any signs of suspicious activity. I needed to go outside and confer with my captain.

I told the new soldier to stay inside and guard the man, in case he tried to run away. "Do not shoot," I warned. "You can break his nose if you need to, but do not shoot him."

I had barely crossed the threshold, my stride assertive as I sought out my captain, when I heard a gunshot. The sound reverberated from inside the house, shattering my thoughts. I spun around and dashed inside, where the Iraqi man lay crumpled on the floor, a bullet hole draining the blood from his heart.

The little girl was distraught, screaming, "Baba, Baba, Baba!" Her cries for her daddy went unheard, while her mother clamored into the room, hysterical.

"Why did you shoot him?" I grilled the soldier, already leery of his history of misconduct.

The renegade soldier claimed that the man had moved toward him, supposedly reaching toward the rifle that he was holding. It was all a matter of perception, an impulsive assumption misaligned with the mental state of the feeble resident. The soldier was wrong in precipitating, and he later received an Article 15 non-judicial punishment for his foolish act. But even though he was disciplined by the military, the damage had already been done in that home, resulting in one more widow, one more orphan.

My own heart spilled over with grief, a flood of compassion for the tiny girl who had watched her father die of a needless gunshot wound. She was too young to experience this trauma, and even at my age, I could not fathom how I would have felt if I had watched as the men shot my father in Samarra. A yearning washed over my spirit, a longing to comfort the distraught girl and her mother. My characteristic callousness was gone. I had always been a thick-skinned soldier, a sniper who could stare down the barrel at any target and feel no sorrow, hell-bent on proving to the insurgents and even the local population that they were shameful people. I did not want to waste any energy with compassion for the contemptible community of rebels who disrespected the US military and oppressed their own people. But God had clearly stirred my heart. He was changing my broken life, touching me with a hand that exists to exhibit mercy to the undeserving. I realized in that moment that although I had been as vile as anyone else, God was making me a man who could finally be an agent of love. I was accustomed to following military orders, and now I also wanted to obey the words of Jesus: "This is my command. Love each other" (John 15:17).

As we left the area in a helicopter, the distressed, watery eyes of the little girl still staring in my consciousness, I wished that I could send a shower of kindness to soften her pain. Because of a haphazard bullet, she was now fatherless. If only she could find the same heavenly Father who had reached out to me through the death and life of his son Jesus. If only she could know that same love. My reflections were shaken when dissidents began firing at our helicopter, and I instinctively prayed, asking God to guard my life. I did not want to die. Life was just now beginning.

How fitting that this was my last mission on the Baqubah campaign, a brutal battle that was largely successful on a grander scale, securing the city and laying the groundwork for renewal of the region. As we concluded Operation Arrowhead Ripper on August 19, 2007, the territory of Baqubah and the Diyala province as a whole were in better condition upon our exit than when we had entered in June. The strenuous summer was also the setting for my own rebirth. I was emerging better than I had ever been, because of what God had done within me. The spiritual victory was tangible, while simultaneously I was facing an earthly struggle of my own.

CHAPTER SEVENTEEN

I was the sniper who survived. Between the 2005 car bomb in Tikrit and the Battle of Baqubah in the summer of 2007, I had escaped senseless IED attacks and dodged more bullets than the seeds in the pomegranates in our yard back home. I had pulled the trigger countless times, not to keep a personal score but to contribute to the wartime cause to the best of my abilities. I wanted to see a land where torture, bloodshed, and exploitation were no more than a vanishing memory, where instead, harmony and honor could be more than a vaporous wish. No projectiles had shredded my flesh; no provocations had tattered my mind. I was the strong sniper who survived, and now I was learning to give the credit to God. I was confident that I had served the US military with excellence, and yet my footing on Iraqi soil was unsteady.

I was on a most-wanted list. My father would have been proud of my accomplishments, and yet I was in danger of meeting his same fate. I was an Iraqi traitor, so they would say. I had willfully aided the infidel, putting myself on the side of the US in a conflict that attacked the corrupt sociopolitical fabric of my homeland. Because of this, my name was put in print in a place where it did not belong, on a list of torturous doom as if I were disloyal to my native Iraq, the country I was striving to salvage. The terrorists, who saw only my uniform and not my dutiful motives, wanted to eliminate me, just as they had done to my father for his spy activities.

I knew that my days were numbered because a sister US military unit in Baiji, Iraq, had apprehended a terrorist and discovered a glaring piece of paper in his pocket. It was a list of the people whom he and his cohorts wanted to capture, and I was the tenth name. The first five names had already been crossed off the list, so the prowlers were surely on the loose, ready to pounce on me without warning.

My American dream to live in the US was now an Iraqi necessity. Long ago, I had adopted the nickname Tex with a sense of casual longing for the open country that seemed so attractive, an idyllic destination where the horizon was as wide as the opportunities. Now the daydream was a nightmare, not that my desire to live in the US had diminished at all. But now, my longings were agitated by a hair-raising chase. I needed to go there, far from the haunting landscapes of Iraq where my identity was a death sentence.

I returned with the troops to Tikrit only long enough to pack my bags. The US military leadership acted on my behalf to solicit a rightful passage, allowing me access to US immigration and citizenship documentation on the basis of my performance as an Iraqi interpreter. Only a select few interpreters were granted this type of clemency within the parameters of the immigration program. The men who had direct authority over me on the ground had observed my dedication and were willing to advocate, vouching for my integrity, putting their own careers at risk in order to assert that I had no intention of being an undercover Iraqi rebel on US territory. Although I had already expressed the desire to go to the US and had even begun the application process in the previous months, the entire situation became accelerated when everyone realized the urgency of my status. I flew to Baghdad the next day.

It took two trips and a lot of determination. The first time I arrived at the US embassy in the Green Zone in Baghdad, the international hub for the Coalition Provisional Authority, the consular officers told me that they could not help me. There was an unforeseen delay, a gap in the paper trail, a pause that shortened the distance between me and the terrorists whose handwritten lists were all too well organized. I needed to cross the border, not get stuck in a bureaucratic blockade. Frustrated, I returned to Tikrit, knowing that my name was scribbled on a most-wanted list that might still be circulating, while I was stranded without a passport.

Two days later, I returned to Baghdad with the US military sergeant who had overseen my final mission in Baqubah, and we got lost in the Yellow Zone, where safety was anything but guaranteed. After a short-lived but scary detour, we found the embassy, succeeding in obtaining approval for the final phase of my passport. Along the way, we came across a group of Christian people from Sudan, who started dancing and singing when I told them that I had just put my trust in Jesus as my Savior. While I was desperately running for my life, waiting for the embassy to finalize my documentation, their celebration uplifted me, reminding me that my life was ultimately secure. The words were in a dialect that I did not know, and yet the spirit of their lyrics beat in tune with my heart. I had just emerged from the furnace of wartime, where casualties surrounded me in the smoldering heat, and the elation of these Sudanese Christians was so foreign to me. At the same time, there was a familiarity to their joy, reminiscent of what Jesus had said to his followers about troubled times: "I have told you these things, so that in me you may have peace. In this world you will have trouble. But take heart! I have overcome the world" (John 16:33).

I needed to hold onto that hope, a stronghold for my mixed emotions. Finally, the US embassy in Amman, Jordan, sent an indication that my immigration clearance was in good standing. Buoyed up by that good news, I still had one more hurdle to overcome before leaving Iraq. It was time to say goodbye to my family. My mother and two of my younger siblings came to the Green Zone in Baghdad, a send-off that was anything but jubilant without my father among us. His absence sucked the warmth out of each hug.

My mother's hardy arms enveloped me, her melodically mournful voice encouraging me that I would have a better life outside of Iraq. Crossing the border to bypass the terrorists' clutch was not an act of cowardice or betrayal. It was essential. She expressed great satisfaction in having a son who was a valiant soldier, a young man who could brave battles and borders while upholding the family's reputation of warring for peace. I went with her blessing, and with one final command.

"Call us," she said, as I reluctantly pulled away and braced myself to leave. I nodded in agreement, not wanting to take the chance that my voice might shake. I had never traveled outside of Iraq, and while it seemed so momentous, my excitement did not allow me to ignore the uncertainties ahead. I knew that I could never return to Iraq. I wondered what fresh flavors awaited me on the other side of the sea, while also wondering if I would ever again taste my mother's homemade kleicha cookies.

CHAPTER EIGHTEEN

The flight from Baghdad to Amman was speedy and direct, transporting me like a sandgrouse darting to a source of water in the desert. I needed to avoid predators and attain an oasis that I hoped was not a false mirage. One of my former SWAT instructors was preparing the way for me in the US, providing a place to stay—I just had to get there without becoming the prey of a terrorist.

Upon landing in Amman, the border patrol officials were suspicious of me at first glance but allowed me entry when they recognized that I had documents to back up my progression to Jordan. The city's seven hills offered me high ground, a secure vantage point to gear up for my transcontinental adventure. I needed to stay in the capital while embassy officials completed my paperwork, and I immediately felt safer, far from the strain of war, far from vulnerable exposure in the desert plains of Iraq. I had $15,000 in a bank account and rented a furnished condo for one week while I waited for the final seal of approval from the embassy.

It was an impromptu vacation minus the merriment, since I was on my own and had nothing to do except wait. I explored the city, sightseeing and eating in restaurants, where the falafel and hummus did not tantalize my taste buds like the food I had always eaten at home. But I was content, even if slightly uneasy whenever the thought crossed my mind that the US was a big country where I had no family and no certain future. At least in the foggy hills of Amman, my nightmare was looking a little more like a dream again. Tex—and Texas—meant a land of opportunity, and Jordan was an extended layover, getting me closer to the nation whose flag I had defended for so many months.

The taxi driver who had picked me up at the airport became my companion for the week, transporting me around the city, glad to be a guide for an Iraqi soldier who had dinars to spend. We went to bars, and as the visiting Iraqi gentleman, I covered the $400 tab for some Russian girls as well. I blew $5,000 right away, only realizing in retrospect that the taxi driver was overcharging me to his own advantage. At one restaurant, he increased my bill by $500 and pocketed the change. Apparently, I was savvier as a sniper than as a tourist, but at least my life was no longer at stake.

On September 28, 2007, I flew from Jordan to the United States of America, landing in San Antonio, Texas. Gliding over the vast ocean in a long-winded airplane, where the insistent hum of the engine was more monotonous and pacifying than the blunt, edgy sound of Apache helicopter blades, I jetted from the quaking terra firma of war to what I hoped would be a reliable place of peace. My SWAT instructor friend and his wife were waiting to host me, their gesture of hospitality so pervasive and genuine that I considered them my American parents. The instructor had taken me under his wing right from the start during my initial integration to the SWAT team. I was a skinny recruit at the time, trying desperately to beef up my muscles and prove to everyone, and even to myself, that I was as much a man as the best of them.

Once, when I was originally learning how to shoot, the instructor took me to the range, handed me a 9mm pistol, and said, "If you put all your bullets in one hole, I will buy you a month's supply of protein supplements." I did it. He was surprised, and he fulfilled his word. He stocked me with protein, building my strength and serving as a conduit for my growth. Now I did not need him to teach me the secret skills of a sniper—I needed something more fundamental. I needed a bed, a pillow, a place to call home.

I was excited—I was becoming Tex of Texas. It was nighttime

when we pulled away from the San Antonio airport, heading toward their house about twenty minutes outside of the city. I was instinctually on alert since most of the Iraqi insurgent attacks on soldiers happened in the shroud of darkness, and we never knew what bump in the road might be concealing an IED. Too many of those crazy episodes had killed men, and I was accustomed to ensuring the safety of my instructor in all of our comings and goings on the roadways of Iraq. So, as we drove along the open highway, I maintained a casual conversation about my fifteen hour flight from Amman, the short layover in Chicago, and the two-hour hop into San Antonio, while watching the scenery with a trained eye.

Suddenly, I saw two trash bags planted on the side of the highway, huddled masses like the ones that often cloaked explosives, a hurried sprinkling of sand tricking a passerby into thinking that they had been tossed aside as rubbish instead of deposited there for destruction. "Watch those bags!" I yelled. "Watch those bags!"

"Hey, calm down," my instructor said, his foot steady on the gas pedal. "There are no bombs here."

No bombs. It sounded idyllic, if only I knew how to live without war, without constantly wondering if there was an insurgent around the next corner. I had no classic symptoms of Post-Traumatic Stress Disorder, unlike many wounded warriors who wage a mental battle long after they leave the theater of war. My mind was stable, my body was uninjured, my heart was renewed by my faith in Jesus. In my compact luggage, I carried the small Bible that I had picked up from the shelf, its pages already more yellowed after just one summer, its words of life already a treasure more precious than any of the trophy knives that some soldiers sought.

Getting acclimated in the US was no fanciful fairy tale, however. It was a new culture, and I had no occupation. To begin, I was drowsy from jetlag, having breached many houses and performed many night missions but never having crossed a time zone until flying halfway around the globe. It was disorienting, and it started the following day with a surprise celebration. My hosts threw a party in my honor, inviting their friends to welcome me to a land where the red, white, and blue of independence are the fiber of society. The diversified crowd was overwhelming. The guest list of any party in Iraq is naturally a throng of relatives, not an assortment of unrelated friends, so I thought it strange not to observe a tight kinship among people. I would have to create my own family bonds in this country.

A few weeks later, my surrogate father and former SWAT instructor was deployed to his next private contractor job, a six-month commitment which left me staying alone with his wife. I was still a novice in the US, with no means of transportation to explore the San Antonio area nor the audacity to search for employment. Immigration had been successful, but without a career I was aimless. I stayed at the house, wearing the high-cut boyish shorts that were the norm among soldiers, unaware that my leisurewear was inappropriate around my instructor's wife. The days were a bore, but I helped with chores and managed to stay out of trouble even though I had too much free time.

Although my faith had not dwindled, it had no environment to develop. There was no one to teach me, no church community to embrace my fledgling commitment to follow God. One highlight during this period was a visit from Sgt. Gray, who had shown me how to read the Bible, leading me to an understanding of the ways of Jesus while close to the front lines in Baqubah. He and his wife, who had also served in Iraq, came to Houston to visit her parents and traveled to San Antonio to see me. It was a prized reunion, strolling along the River Walk and stopping at the Alamo while reminiscing about the combat that had compelled us to be friends for life. The church pastor who had been praying for me also lived in San Antonio, so they took me to meet him briefly. Even though the church was too far across the city for me to access on my own, it was gratifying to know that a man who had prayed for me from afar was now close by, a brother in the family of God.

Shortly after that, I suggested to my instructor's wife that perhaps I could go live with her brother, twenty minutes away, eliminating the awkwardness of sharing such close quarters with a married woman who was not mine. She had been gracious to allow me to remain at the house, but I sensed that it was better to find a room where I could feel more comfortable. Everyone agreed, and I was glad to have a place to go where I could talk with another man and get advice about prospects for employment. Even better, my instructor's brother-in-law was also a war veteran, so we immediately drilled down into military lingo and discussed my possibilities for reenlistment. He was retired from the US Army, having become a wildland firefighter, and suggested that I could do something similar, working as a firefighter or pursuing a position in the police force. However, he recommended that I consider the US Army, an atmosphere where I could stand tall and serve the flag of the country that had adopted me.

The lifestyle I developed in the country that had allowed me to immigrate was grittier than I had anticipated, going against the norms of my background. My veteran host had the habit of going to bars on the weekends, and I tagged along, having nothing else to occupy my attention. I was utterly unprepared for the interactions that happened at these raucous hangouts, the coquettish women, the exhilarating drinks, the rash excursions. Whether it was the novelty of mind-bending alcohol or the latent desires of a soldier who was finally free from the rules of engagement, I am not sure. I made some poor decisions.

One night, I got sick of who I was becoming. I had escaped the threat of death in Iraq, yet I was rotting on the inside, running in the wrong direction on the path of life. Wild ruin awaited me. The realization overcame me like a flare in the sky, jolting my outlook and illuminating the dark recesses of my disposition with sparks that tinged my conscience. I prayed, asking God to put me among people who cared more about seeking his face in all of its bright glory than partying with pretty faces in shadowy bars. What I needed was not entertainment. I wanted someone who could teach me more about this God to whom I had entrusted my entire life.

Within two days, a military recruiter called me. After a series of delays in which my earnest desire to enlist had not been taken seriously and I was aggravated by my poor results in the ASVAB aptitude test, the recruitment officers had heeded the advice of my host. Although my instructor's brother-in-law was not a fantastic social influence on me, he wanted the best for my career. As a veteran himself, he had called the recruitment captain on my behalf, urging the military to give me a chance. His backing was the impetus that I had lacked in order to advance, and I was grateful.

When I received the call, not only was I accepted but also the offer required moving halfway across the country, leaving Texas, the place where my dreams were only starting to come true. The big state of Texas had welcomed me warmly, fulfilling my initial aspiration to live up to my name as Tex, but I needed more than food and shelter. I did not come to Texas to be a lone star, a former sniper who had lost his luster. I needed a home and a purpose, an occupation in this land of opportunity so that I could carry on the honor of my family name. Jesus had promised to his followers a journey full of light, out of the recesses of darkness, ready to ignite others to walk in the right path of goodness. "I am the light of the world," Jesus said. "Whoever follows me will never walk in darkness, but will have the light of life" (John 8:12). I was ready to walk forward.

CHAPTER NINETEEN

There was a spot for me in Fort Jackson, South Carolina, and I departed from San Antonio on February 18, 2008, to claim my position in basic combat training for the US Army. When I arrived at the base, I was pulled aside from the larger group of recruits and funneled into a company of multinational interpreters and translators, including three other Iraqis. Since dusk had already fallen, I received my gear with instructions to locate my bunk and go to sleep. I always picked the top bunk, disgusted by the idea of another man sleeping above me, where any dust and grime might gravitate downward on my mattress or, worse, my face. I dozed off, tired from the trip but not wanting to miss anything in the adventure ahead.

"Get up! Get up!" three sergeants shouted. It was 4:00 a.m. when they rushed into the barracks, startling all of us and yanking the sheets off the beds. There is no room for complacency or comfort in the army, and a bare mattress strips away smug convenience, demanding attention. We had ten minutes to appear at formation, where we stood in a line for a rigid roll call before initiating what would become a morning stretching routine, followed by one or two hours of physical education. We ran extensively, did bear crawls so backbreaking that they insulted our dignity, and then bounced our way through jumping jacks, push-ups, and sit-ups until every muscle grunted.

The regimen dictated a five-minute breakfast in the mess hall, a slightly frenetic but still orderly dash for sustenance that we repeated at lunch and dinner. Between greasy grilled cheese sandwiches, quesadillas that were neither Tex nor Mex, and mounds of corn, the American equivalent of the barley that stocks every Iraqi cupboard except without the pungent turmeric flavor, I was not enticed by the menu. The cakes and puddings looked more appealing, so I learned to start with dessert and satisfy my hunger in four minutes and fifty-nine seconds.

For the following nine months, in addition to the physical exercise, I attended English and math classes. I excelled in English, already familiar with the language and happy to expand my skills in reading and writing. Math, on the other hand, was a complex vortex of calculations and diagrams, and I hated it. To make matters worse, the officers assigned so many chores that I struggled to find time to study. Stripping and waxing the floors on my hands and knees was not what I had envisioned when I enlisted for the army, and I detested the daily grind.

My bad attitude stemmed from my negative view of the authorities who surrounded me on base. None of the drill sergeants had ever been deployed, so I disrespected their untested notions of how to succeed in combat. They seemed to resent my solid experience, not wanting to hear my perspective as a sniper who had completed intense missions and who happened to be a native Iraqi. While my résumé could have been an instructive tool to enhance the training of the new recruits, it seemed to intimidate more than spark interest. I sensed that they were trying to weed me out of the field by not giving me a spare minute to study. Since I was not treated with the consideration that I thought I deserved, I talked back to the sergeants, getting into further trouble for cussing and smoking. I snuck off the base on the weekends, claiming that I was going to the chapel and then venturing farther away to cavort like any soldier, never getting caught. On a few weekends, Sgt. Gray visited me from North Carolina, showing up by surprise and keeping me from losing sight of my goal to let Jesus be the light of my life. I always welcomed his guidance, his unswerving example of allowing the words of the Bible to inspire his every thought and action. When I was with him, those words were a delight, a breath of fresh air in the drudgery of army assignments.

In September 2008, after months of physical training and classroom instruction, I had to take an examination similar to the entrance test, to prove that my skills had advanced. Much to my frustration, I failed by one point because of my difficulty in mastering the mathematical portion of the exam. I begged permission to take the test again, determined to become eligible for a career in the army. There were a few recruits from Sudan who had failed by two or three points, and yet the captain had favored them, brushing me aside.

I pleaded my case to the presiding captain, crying tears of desperation. If only I could have a second chance, I could proceed and serve America. There was nothing else that I wanted to do with my life. "No," the captain said, her tone terse and unconvinced. "You are done."

CHAPTER TWENTY

The land of opportunity was becoming a marsh of misfortune.
The sunny days of learning to swim in the swampy waters of
the Tigris River seemed like a distant memory of another life. I had
gasped to stay afloat then, and now my circumstances were just
as sodden, weighed down as I flailed my arms, getting nowhere.
Disoriented, I could not call out for my older brother Babr to
rescue me, pulling me out of the raging waters of confusion, nor
would I trouble my mother with my disappointments. Besides,
she was difficult to reach, as she kept changing phone numbers in
her own attempt to stay well in Iraq. And, of course, my father had
already become a victim of his own fight for survival. I lived as if I
had no family.

I remembered that Sgt. Gray had always treated me with true
kindness, saying that we were brothers in our faith. This love
between Christians, he taught me, is a bond that endures all things,
based on the love of Jesus, who had said, "As I have loved you, so
you must love one another" (John 13:34). Although I did not want
to admit that I was defeated, I knew that I needed my friend's help
to gain victory over the obstacles of settling in the US, this country
where every opportunity was an overwhelming challenge.

Calling Sgt. Gray, who was still stationed in North Carolina
after his return from Iraq, I explained that I had lost the possibility
of pursuing an army career. I knew that returning to Texas would
be an error, as it was not an environment conducive to who I
wanted to be. I may have demonstrated a tendency to swerve,

making mistakes along the way, but my desire was to be a good man, honoring God. Sgt. Gray rose to the occasion beyond my expectations, insisting that I come live with him and his wife for a while. Within a few days, he picked me up partway in Columbia, South Carolina, taking me to his house in Fayetteville, North Carolina, to discover a fresh path in the sandhills region near Fort Bragg. The pine trees differed from the palm trees of Iraq, the sandy soil nothing like the desert dunes where I had once herded my father's sheep, but the warmth of their hospitality assured me that I had found a welcoming atmosphere.

I soon became a part-time private contractor, assisting the US military by training Special Forces cadets and other units in a camp setting. I flourished, satisfied to finally be able to pass along my firsthand wartime experience to others who would carry the baton into the future. I could never go back and join the battle, but I could at least contribute to the success of ambitions that I embraced. The theater of war had been a crucial component in my personal development, but not as an end in itself. It was an enterprise designed to improve the lives of people who, although foreign like myself, were worthy of a secure and peaceful existence.

More significant than my professional development, I started to attend Bible studies with Sgt. Gray on Tuesday evenings. The group gathered to read and discuss the teachings of Jesus, applying the principles to daily life in a practical way. Not only did I read more sections of the Bible than I had perused in Iraq, I memorized many verses, fascinated with how the ancient writings fit my present reality. I marked my place with paper clips, logging my progress with military precision. "I have been crucified with Christ and I no longer live, but Christ lives in me. The life I now live in the body, I live by faith in the Son of God, who loved me and gave himself for me" (Galatians 2:20). I had entrusted my life to God while crouched on a roof in the Battle of Baqubah, and I knew that my body had withstood the car bomb in Tikrit for a reason. Because Jesus had died, I was alive.

Once I was exhibiting signs that I was stable, striving, and strong, Sgt. Gray gently nudged me to move into a nearby bachelor pad with eight other young men who were also believers in Jesus. When he and his wife pushed me out of the nest, it was not heartless at all. They simply wanted to provide circumstances where I could stand on my own two feet and then soar. The Apache helicopter expeditions were a thing of the past, but I was ready for higher altitudes and needed to exercise the courage and faith that had gotten me this far.

While living in the bachelor pad for an extended period of time, we conducted Bible studies several days a week, and I began to help other soldiers who were seeking spiritual direction. Some of the cadets would go to a local twenty-four hour military shoppette that sold packaged snacks and cigarettes. They would flock there mostly to stock up on alcohol, and I would go there purely to share the truth of Jesus with them. It was easy for me to earn their trust, as I understood their wandering lusts, but for me those passions were a part of my past. Sometimes they asked for advice that caught me by surprise.

"Would you like to come to JFK Memorial Chapel to learn about Jesus?" one of my Bible study buddies asked a cadet one evening at the shoppette while I was standing next to them.

"Where is the nearest strip club?" the soldier asked in return, hushed but uninhibited, ready to down a few bottles of beer and lay hands on a good time.

"No," my buddy replied firmly. "We cannot help you with that."

My footing was firm, my faith not swayed. After about three years at the bachelor pad, I moved in with two other Christian men who were in military training courses. They were solid companions, teaching me more about the Holy Spirit of God. I had been so engrossed with the knowledge of God as my eternal Father and Jesus as the Son who had sacrificed his life in my place, that I had never learned about the Spirit. They showed me in the Bible how Jesus had promised not to leave us alone, to lead us forever in righteousness. "When he, the Spirit of truth, comes, he will guide you into all truth" (John 16:13). I was amazed, understanding what I had been missing, and my roommates enjoyed teasing me that they could see smoke coming out of my head whenever I had a spiritual realization.

These well-groomed young men helped me to make the transition from the posture of a military hero to a proper citizen, capable of functioning in the larger community. I was accustomed to the more straightforward language among soldiers, and they counseled me to remember the polite subtleties of saying "please" and "thank you." Not that I was trying to impress anyone. I had chosen to give up dating for nine months, sensing that God wanted to mold my spiritual maturity before allowing me to immerse myself in any relationship with a young woman. I looked at it as a fast, just like a person might deprive themselves of food in order to clear their inner being. In my case, I was motivated by a sincere desire to become the man whom Jesus wanted me to be, avoiding any distraction.

In November 2011, I was confident that my dating fast had ended and that God would look upon me with favor if I searched for a lovely young lady to join me in the journey of life. Far away from the norms of Iraqi culture and the traditions of previous generations, I was on my own with no arranged marriage or formalized introductions orchestrated by my relatives. My father was not able to seek a suitable bride for me, and without his advice available, I needed an alternative. I decided to register on a Christian dating website with a reputation for being reliable, not rash. Posting a photograph, I drafted my profile with a smooth combination of honesty and flair. I was up-front that I had been in the military, though I wanted to ease into the shock factor that I had been a sniper. Any woman needed to know that, and yet I also wanted to appear likable, authentic, a man whose heart was as tender as his uniform was tough.

This was unfamiliar territory, trying to meet a good woman in this odd country where all the ladies seemed so bold, smiling freely and shamelessly making eye contact with strangers. The website was a safer starting point, and immediately a profile caught my attention. Michelle had deep brown eyes that conveyed a gentle spirit, and yet the description she had written made it obvious to me that she was courageous enough not to be scared of a sniper. I emailed her, and we corresponded back and forth for a few days. Unlike any other woman, she intrigued me, asking questions about my background and evidencing genuine interest in me as a person. A sensation of peace overcame me, as if I had settled into an extraordinary place in this land that was so foreign. Because I was slightly self-conscious, not confident that my written English was fluent, I asked if we could talk on the phone. I had served as an interpreter, not a translator of formal documents, so I felt much more at ease in conversation. She agreed to take my call.

One call turned into many, and we developed a delightful long-distance friendship throughout the following two months. Pretty soon, the distance seemed to be too much. I was still living in Fayetteville, North Carolina, while she was in Lancaster County, Pennsylvania, so I suggested that we meet somewhere in the middle. We agreed to meet in Richmond, Virginia, on February 12, 2012, just two days shy of Valentine's Day. On my way there, I stopped at a Jared jewelry store, asking the sales associate for a recommendation of an item to purchase for a first date with a special young woman. She responded that girls usually like necklaces and earrings, showing me an option that sparkled just like I imagined Michelle's eyes. The jewelry set cost a staggering $300, but I bought it anyway, sure that it was not money wasted. I would have spent even more on her, as money means nothing compared to the value of life.

I arrived at the Science Museum of Virginia in an executive suit, ready to make the best possible impression, and my hopes were not dashed. Michelle was even more lovely in person, and the magnetism and chemistry between us were not a mere result of the scientific museum. After exploring the exhibits, we went to eat at The Cheesecake Factory. I presented the jewelry, hardly noticing the delicious meal on my plate while I watched Michelle's expressions throughout our conversation. Buoyed up by the day's positive experiences, I asked if she would be my girlfriend. There was no reluctance in her trusting gaze.

From February to October, we saw each other once a month in Fayetteville, Lancaster, or halfway in between, talking on the phone every day and via Skype on weekends. As the weeks passed, it made less and less sense to be so far apart. Wanting to eliminate the goodbyes and always have Michelle by my side, I proposed to her at Greenfield Park in Lancaster on October 13, 2012. The soft spray of a fountain was the perfect background for my simple, sincere question and her happy "yes." Finally, my cross-country trek had brought me to a resting place, a relationship, the prospect of establishing a home with someone I loved.

CHAPTER TWENTY-ONE

As Tex, I had always longed to live in Texas, and I had done it. My given name, Abbas, means father in Arabic, and I was ready to live up to that identity as well. Michelle and I married on April 27, 2013. Soon, I would have a new family of my own, far from my native Iraq, and yet near to my heart.

We settled in Lancaster County, Pennsylvania, where Michelle was already employed as a social worker and where I got a job at a tire company after submitting just one application. As I was selling tires for cars of all kinds, the horse-drawn Amish buggies that I passed on the narrow roads were miles apart from the Humvees that had shuttled me across the desert plains of battle. The sturdy, green cornfields that overspread the serene countryside contrasted distinctly with the sandstone spiral of the minaret in my hometown of Samarra at what was once the largest Muslim mosque in the world. So many church steeples speckled the Lancaster County hills and valleys, reminding me of my Christian faith and, with it, my responsibility to tell others about how God had changed my life. The differences between my former home in Iraq and my new one in the US were endless, and yet in my mind and heart I could reconcile the two, finding links of commonality from a human and eternal perspective. I may have left Iraq, but my departure did not pull away my roots. If anything, I was transplanted, given the opportunity to flourish in another land where I could learn more about Jesus, who had saved me physically in battle and spiritually for eternity.

I was thriving and more than satisfied, grateful to know God as my Father, and grateful to become a father alongside my wife, Michelle. We named our first child, a son, Asher, meaning happy or blessed, and we named our daughter Grace, a testament to all of the goodness that I received but did not deserve. Both of those names represent the beginning of a fresh heritage of faith. Aside from "father," my name also means "lion," which may seem fitting for a strong-willed sniper, a SWAT team member who knows how to breach houses and batter rough rebels.

However, when I reflect on my military service and the miraculous way that I did not become a target of any of the stealthy explosions that nearly extinguished my breath, I remember those first perplexing verses that I read in the Bible. The words about sheep were repulsive to me initially, but then my curiosity could not resist the thought. I am more like a sheep than a lion. Wandering aimlessly astray like the sheep that I used to lead in Ad-Dawr seems a lot more natural than roaring like the lions of ancient Iraq that adorned symbols of Babylon. As Jesus said, "I am the good shepherd; I know my sheep and my sheep know me" (John 10:14). I found the Shepherd, or the Shepherd found me. The name of Jesus spoke to my spirit on the day when my body was thrust into the air by a car bomb that, by all accounts, should have decimated me. And now, when I recall the miserably injured victims of the car bomb, bloodied and lining the hallway of the hospital in Tikrit, their cries reverberate in my mind like the bleating of sheep. They, and the other people of Iraq, are like lost sheep who need guidance. Because God loved me enough to guide me to safety, I want to do the same for others.

Jesus said to his follower Peter, "'Do you love me?'

He answered, 'Yes, Lord, you know that I love you.'

Jesus said, 'Take care of my sheep'" (John 21:16).

While I was once a man who wielded a powerful rifle, now I am an agent of peace. While I was once as unyielding as the sandstone minaret in Samarra, now I have a heart filled with compassion.

Only God could have done this, transforming me to become a man who knows Jesus. "I will give you a new heart and put a new spirit in you; I will remove from you your heart of stone and give you a heart of flesh" (Ezekiel 36:26).

I am still a sheep. I still need the Shepherd to lead me all the way. On my own, I could have become as bad or worse than the people whose hostile activities I despised. "Once you were alienated from God and were enemies in your minds because of your evil behavior. But now he has reconciled you by Christ's physical body through death to present you holy in his sight, without blemish and free from accusation" (Colossians 1:21-22). Because I picked up a Bible that someone had tossed aside on a shelf in the middle of the Iraq War, I learned more than a few catchy phrases in English. I learned truth that captured my heart and gave me a triumph that means more than any battle victory. And now I am poised to serve not as an Arabic interpreter, but as a man who can tell others anywhere about Jesus.

I am not a sniper with nothing more than a tally of kills. I am the sniper saved by grace who survived with a story of life. I do not talk about my kill count. What counts most to me is survival in a larger story that lasts forever.

Abbas Hameed was born in Samarra, Iraq and lived in the country for 23 years. During the Operation Iraqi Freedom, the United States military was looking for Iraqi's who were bilingual in Arabic and English. Abbas was bilingual and had an interest in assisting the military, so he signed up to be an interpreter.

At the beginning of 2005, Abbas was hit by a car bomb while on duty. He was the only survivor. This made him start to seek for Jesus Christ and answers.

Abbas searched for two years for someone to teach him how to read the Bible. Finally, he found a friend in the military who explained how to read the Bible to him. Abbas started to read the Bible every day. Within a year, Abbas accepted Jesus Christ as his Lord and Savior.

Currently, Abbas lives in Lancaster County, Pennsylvania with his wife, Michelle and their two children, Asher and Grace.

To learn more about Hameed Christian Ministries, to order more copies of this book, and to schedule Abbas Hameed for a speaking engagement, please visit the following website.

www.hameedchristianministries.com

Please use the following address to contact Abbas Hameed by mail:

Abbas Hameed
Hameed Christian Ministries
P.O. Box 306
Akron, PA 17501-0306